PHILOSOPHER'S STONE

Unraveling The Mind's Mysteries
To Unleash Your Limitless Potential

SIVANESWARAN

ISBN 979-8-88975-540-1

DEDICATION

This book is a tribute to the insults, failures, rejections, and struggles that have shaped my journey, allowing me to become the person I am today. Each trial and tribulation has been a profound lesson, unveiling a world of endless possibilities.

To the unrelenting voice in my head that will never allow me to stop.

CONTENTS

AUTHOR'S NOTE

I choose you, Aladdin.

The phase you exist should puzzle and astonish you. You and I and every other living creature are machines of inexpressible complexity, the complexity of a magnitude that is a challenge to humanity. The scope of human life and its quest for happiness is astounding. Life is mind-shattering to anyone who truly grasps it. I have aimed to put together some remarks which are inspired by what I hope is insightful in understanding life.

This book lets you think for yourself, discourages you from falling into stereotypical and habitual traps and pokes fun at conventional thoughts which may hold you back.

The intended readers of this book will find joy in reading, tolerance for differences, and happiness in discovering new things that will set them free from primitive common beliefs.

This book is not addressed to the learned and those who regard a practical problem merely as something to be talked about.

Let the journey begin!

CHAPTER -1

SNOOZE

NEWTON'S APPLE

Once upon a time in the faubourg of England, during autumn, the trees look pretty and dazzle in their golden-brown cover. The leaves appear bright and reddish-orange as the wind gusts through each swaying tree, tossing apples till they're free. Young Isaac Newton rests beneath an apple tree contemplating the mysterious universe. Suddenly an apple hits him on the head.

"Voilá !" he shouts.

In a flash, he understands that the very same force that brought the apple crashing toward the ground also keeps the moon falling toward the earth and the earth falling toward the sun i.e. gravity.

If this had happened in the twenty-first century, Isaac Newton would have continued to take multiple snaps of the apple and would have captured beautiful pictures. But he would have cared less for the falling apple.

There are some days when you just feel more powerful. You force yourself to get up early and sweat before everyone else wakes up. That sets the tone for the rest of your day. You feel excited about your life. You feel young, confident, and alive. Everything clicks. You feel like you're going somewhere and like you have momentum.

You become a more powerful version of yourself.

It is the part of you that loves discovery, curiosity, challenge and heading somewhere while talking aloud. It is a force inside you that wants to grow, move and expand. At the same time, there's an equal and opposite force that works to hold you back. Resistance is the force that dwells on your curiosity and growth. It's an inner, evolutionary bias to take the safe bet, the sure thing, and the known path. Whenever you're feeling bored, bummed, or broken, your power is off and resistance is on.

Newton's first law of motion states that an object either remains at rest or continues to move at a constant velocity unless acted upon by an external force.

Procrastination is a fundamental law of the universe. It is Newton's first law applied to productivity. Objects at rest tend to stay at rest. It works the other way too. Objects in motion tend to stay in motion. When it comes to being productive, the important thing is to find a way to get started. Once you get started, it is much easier to stay in motion.

Resistance loves surfing the web, sticking to the routine, snoozing, avoiding confrontation, and making excuses. It will keep your life in place and the power inside you will push your life forward. You will always feel the tension between these two forces. Every single day of your life, you have the choice to stay where you are or move your life in new directions.

The question is, "Will the powerful you, turn on and start taking action, or will you resist and wait just a little longer to get joy, satisfaction, and fulfilment?"

You decide!

THE LION KING

From childhood, you have been taught that the lion is the king of the jungle. But have you ever wondered why the lion is the king of the jungle?

If you think about it, the lion is not the biggest animal in the jungle, the elephant is. The lion is not even the fastest animal in the jungle. It is the cheetah. So what makes the lion the king of the jungle if he isn't the fastest or the biggest animal?

The most powerful people or rulers of a country are referred to as kings. Perhaps that is why the lion is regarded as the king. He has complete authority over the territory he lives on, as well as all the other animals that reside there. He is known for his bravery. Everything of worth is guarded by the lion. The family, the pride, the jungle, everything!

If you threaten anything that is of value to the lion, you better be prepared to fight. The lion teaches us to be protective of the things that matter to us.

What makes the lion the king of the jungle is his unique mentality. The only distinction between a lion and an elephant is that a lion thinks of food when he sees an elephant whereas an elephant considers escaping. The way a lion thinks is mirrored in his behaviour. Because of this, the lion is respected above all other animals in the realm. Everyone wants to be like the lion because of his mentality.

The lion is certain. He never second-guesses. When he goes in, he goes in a hundred per cent. There is nothing half-hearted about the lion.

Feel motivated!

MOTIVATION WILL FAIL YOU

You know that it's important to stick to your goals but there is something so annoying and fake about all that motivational philosophy.

Do you want to make your dreams come true?

It is time to get motivated!

Sounds familiar?

People pay big bucks for books and courses on how to find and maintain motivation. A cursory Google search is all you need to confirm that motivation is a thriving industry.

Motivation is a big deal. There aren't many things in life that feel better than peak motivation. It feels like riding a wave, sure of your ability to conquer whatever obstacles lie ahead. You start on your mission with the picture of a triumphant ending already in mind.

It's contagious.

People always believe that motivation is critical to getting things done. Without it, how could you ever finish college or learn a new language or make lots of money?

People believe that tapping into this elusive drive is the only way to reach your goals.

But time and again, motivation will let you down. Motivation may have helped you with the initial inspiration, but it will not take you anywhere. Motivation is utterly unreliable. You could be doing everything right only to realise you have been thrown for a loop.

Sounds unfamiliar? Put on your Sherlock cap!

WHY MOTIVATION FAILS

Motivation fails because it is a feeling. That's all!

Feelings and emotions come and go without warning. Feelings fluctuate in intensity and are vulnerable to the elements. If you get tired, stressed, or hungry, those feelings will take precedence, crowding out motivation and sapping your energy. Motivation is very hard to keep up with once you get it.

Motivation is also abstract. It doesn't show you what you need to do. Motivation is great for envisioning an abstract idea of success but not the meticulous planning that goes into success. Without a plan, motivation's daydreams don't get off the ground.

When things go wrong, they set off a domino effect. Each setback saps your energy further, making the next failure more likely.

Motivation cannot be summoned at will. You can't choose to be motivated. You either are or you aren't. Reading motivational quotes or watching motivational YouTube videos doesn't work if you aren't already in the right headspace. When you have time-bound objectives and determined to wait for motivation, it may not happen. You may as well carry on reading.

MOTIVATION IS A DRUG

Motivation is very useful, just like a cup of coffee in the morning. It can get you moving. It is what gets people to go out and buy workout equipment or a pantry full of healthy foods on a whim. It's what drives writers to make proclamations on social media about finishing their novels. It's what gets people to buy courses and join mailing lists.

But that is usually where motivation ends. Once it is gone, it may never come back. If that is all you depend on, that first shot of inspired energy could be for nought.

"Doubling the dose can be dangerous, Follow doctor's or pharmacist advice"

It is why people buy gym memberships and then never show up. It is why people abandon New Year's resolutions by the third week of January. It is why that novel remains unfinished. Motivation is nothing more than an emotional high. If you want your motivation to lead to results, you must pair it with something that lasts longer than an afternoon.

FOCUS ON DETERMINATION

Instead of motivation, put your stock in determination. Determination is the decision to take action and continue to do so despite forces pushing against it. Unlike motivation, your determination is not swayed by emotion and it can be summoned at will. While motivation shows up in short bursts, determination lasts. Here's why.

Determination involves commitment. Determination does not need anything to power it other than a decision. While motivation burns out like a sugar rush, determination, if used properly, doesn't burn out at all. In case it does, you can get it back with a shift in mindset and a renewed commitment.

Determination involves action. When you are determined, you take action even when you don't feel like it. Even when you aren't motivated, your determination is what makes you wake up at 5 am to go to the gym. No sane person is naturally motivated at 5 am.

Determination involves self-discipline. Mistakes won't derail it and neither will difficulty. Determination means showing up and working on your weaknesses. It means powering through the early days when you don't know what the hell you are doing.

Determination involves habits. Habits are the cornerstone of success. Determined people invest in habit-building. Motivation doesn't last long enough to build habits.

This approach, rooted in athletics, is a powerful tool. In a complex and fast-moving business environment, however, it is not a magic pill. For instance, an athlete undergoing training can always go back to the basics on a particularly tough day and come back refreshed on the next, determined to do better. This may not be routinely applicable in other environments.

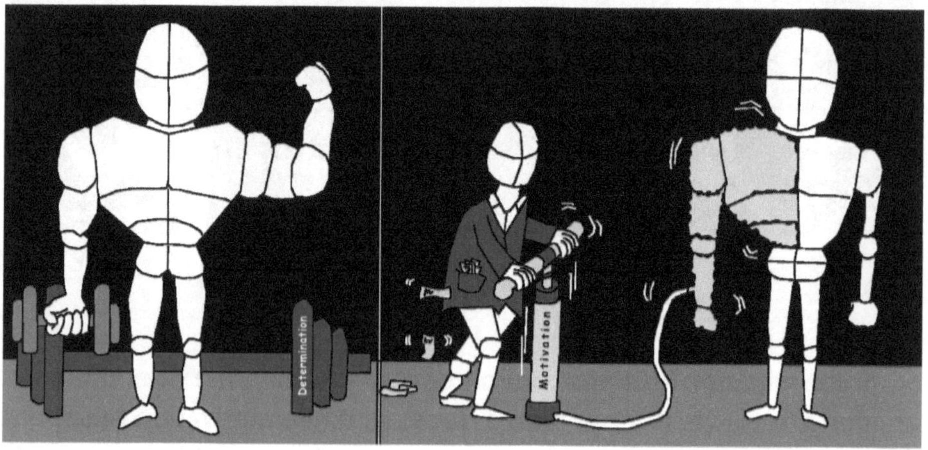

A purpose is bigger than motivation. It's a 'must-do,' not a 'want-to-do.'

Motivation abandons you when the challenges in front of you seem insurmountable. That is the time when you need to question whether you have what it takes. That is when you can turn to your determination. It is a good start, but it's only a start. A true purpose is personal and connecting with it is a journey.

THE SNOOZE BUTTON

It is totally normal to want to hit the snooze button and plenty of us do it. Nothing is inspiring about getting up in the morning. It sucks.

"Whose dumb idea was it to promise to exercise anyway? One day off won't matter that much. Besides, it feels a lot colder today," you mumble.

You close your eyes and feel the welcome sleep overcoming you again. A few minutes later the alarm sounds again and you hit the snooze button once more. You're not feeling up to exercising. Your knee is bothering you again, so it is probably better that you don't push it too hard. Besides, you're going to start exercising tomorrow, so you can give it a solid rest today. You fall asleep again. The alarm rings again. But at this point, it is too late to jog anyway. You hit snooze and drift off again.

While it is not a huge deal to snag a few extra minutes of shut-eye once in a while, fighting your alarm regularly might leave you feeling more tired during the day and sleeping worse at night.

In all of modern history, no single invention has perfectly captured the power of the mind to defeat its own best intentions as the snooze button. Anyone reading this would wonder but procrastination is the only thing between your dreams and your waking life.

The snooze button allows you to delay the inevitable with minimum effort. When you hit the snooze button, you surrender power. Every grand resolution, every good intention, and every promise you've ever made to yourself can be instantly wiped away with a simple press of a button. It allows you to effortlessly delay the real work of changing your life.

Eventually, you snooze your success. The snooze button is the perfect symbol of human resistance. Keep the dreams alive. Hit the snooze button.

WHEN TIME STOPS

The way you react to circumstances determines your feelings. At times you feel like you are drowning in mud. You feel worthless and confused. You want to move, you should, you have to. But you can't and then it evolves into anxiety, fear, and overwhelming emotions.

There are times when life begins to slow down, you feel like doing nothing, and everything slips away. But still, you let it go and watch it go by. Don't you think that this has happened to you many times? Haven't you ignored it thinking you're lazy?

You are not lazy, you are not worthless, and you are not confused. You're 'stuck.'

STUCK

There are times when you know you want more from life but you don't know how to get it and when you tell yourself that you're fine but you really want something more. Sometimes you see the path but don't know the destination—that disturbing feeling is called being stuck.

You get stuck when you think you should be something you are not and when you think that life should be different from what it is. The feeling of being stuck builds slowly from the inside like corrosion on a metal pipe. It is easy to miss because it starts with a vague feeling such as something being a little off.

You feel like something is missing from your life and you can't quite put your finger on what it is, though some words come close—happiness, purpose, excitement, and fun.

Instead of committing yourself to the act, you tend to compromise your ambitions with excuses. They keep you away from your destiny and becoming the person you want to be.

Of course, realising your dreams is not going to be easy. It will require work and commitment from you. But you already know the price of ignoring your dreams far too well. The feeling of being stuck grows stronger inside you and it starts to undermine all aspects of your life.

When you're stuck, the major task is deciding if you're going to change at all. The challenge is finding the ability, in the face of an overwhelming amount of resistance, to create a small change in your life and build on it.

The only way to feel unstuck is to force yourself to change and grow in a meaningful way.

When you are younger, you have all kinds of experiences to look forward to as an adult such as college, moving out on your own, making your own money, blasting music, drinking, travelling, dating, and getting a 'real' job. You are excited about what the future might hold.

The last time you feel that type of optimism is on the eve of your college graduation, anticipating what adult life would be like.

"I'll get out into the real world and get a job where I can travel and manage people," you tell yourself.

But as you grow, your life goes quickly from waiting for something amazing to assuming nothing will. You soon learn that a large part of adult life is robotic work and routine home chores with a bit of happiness.

Deep down, you know why these parts of your life have gone stale. It's because nothing new is happening. You may say that you fear change, but the lack of change in your life is why you feel so empty.

No one can do this for you. You need to push yourself and move forward and grow.

HERMIONE'S FAIRY TALE

Consider the story of Hermione Granger for instance. Back in high school, the studious Hermione was the teacher's pet and most likely to succeed. She met Ron Weasley in college. She felt lost in the sea of students at the big state school and threw herself into the relationship.

Hermione married Ron to get the full value of joy and to share her love with someone. Ron started working for Hogwarts School of Witchcraft and Wizardry and she stayed home. There is nothing like going after your love but Hermione immersed herself in pursuit of love. She created a vacuum by deleting the pages of education, job, success, and the much-needed struggle of life. At some point, she just stopped thinking about what she wanted from her life and figured that this was it.

Occasionally a great novel or a movie like 'Harry Potter' would make her start to think about other possibilities but it didn't last long. She lost the ability to step outside of her routine and see all that life had to offer. She was happy but she always felt that something was missing.

What was she 'missing'?

LOOP

Life's challenges or difficult times can make you feel like you have lost your sense of direction. Deep down though, you probably have a pretty good sense of what you'd like to change.

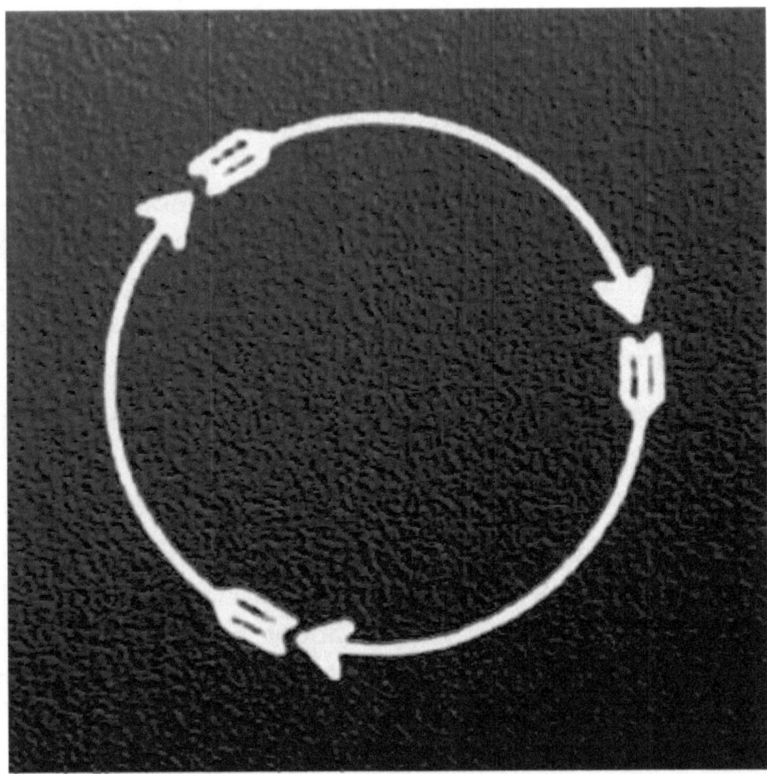

You most likely consider it quite often, not in a fixated, obsessed kind of way, but as a droopy resignation that crosses your mind during the quiet moments when you're alone, like when you are drifting through the supermarket or riding home from work.

You've probably thought about the changes you want to make in your life the way a dog circles a tree full of squirrels. These may include losing eighty pounds, starting a business, proposing your love, building a house, and finding your passion. There's no way you're possibly going to make these changes happen any faster than the dog climbing that tree. You may list a hundred different reasons why, but you keep looking up and checking to see if the squirrels are still there. Sometimes as you circle that tree, you might realise that you're stuck in a loop. You keep making the same resolutions over and over again.

Most people fail to keep their resolutions. That's not unfamiliar to anyone who's made one. You are fired up to hit the gym on January first, but by the morning of the fifth, even those gold stars on the calendar in your closet can't lure you from your warm bed.

You want to change, but you never seem to follow through or you don't ever take the steps to really make it happen. You don't have a clue about what you need to do differently. You've probably tried several times to make a small change but have given up after a few times, gotten side-tracked, or faced too much resistance from others. Or maybe you know your limits too well, so you don't even bother and accept that you are not going to make a change.

The feeling that you are trapped by the life you have created is terrifying. Deep down, you know you want something more, but maybe you don't know what it is or you simply don't have a clue how to get it.

Whether it is fear or frustration or both, the thought of trying to change your life can feel like trying to turn around an eighteen-wheeler in a packed parking lot. Your feelings about it all keep you stuck. If it doesn't 'feel' like a good idea, then you don't do it. That's the problem!

AN OUNCE OF ACTION IS WORTH A TON OF THEORY

It's obvious, right? Take action! But if it is so simple, why don't you take the steps you need to make a change?

Is your modern life very difficult? Or is it your fault you lack the strength, stamina and drive to really be successful?

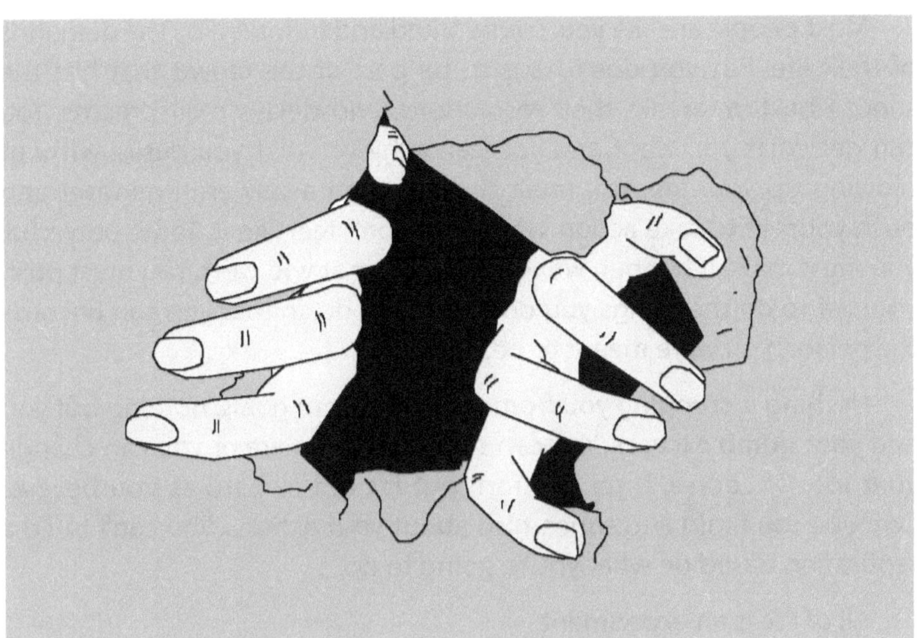

A year from now you may wish you had started today. It is easy to blame the problem on external circumstances such as time, money, or all the little details that get in the way and undercut your energy. There is no doubt that modern life has gotten more complicated.

The uncertainty of life in the twenty-first century can have a big impact on your personal ability and capacity to change. The effort needed to switch from the cell phone to your job is enough to make your mind spin. It may seem as if some of the important stuff is mixed up with all the everyday stuff. You feel as if the direction of your day depends on trivial details such as finding a sock that's missing its mate or forgetting to return a phone call or your spouse's mood at dinner. You have given up on making a serious change in your life, just so you can get through the day.

But the real reason you get stuck has nothing to do with technology or chores, and everything to do with you and who's in charge of your head. You listen to how you feel and stop yourself when you feel afraid or annoyed instead of doing the hard work to transform your desires into something solid and real by taking action.

Most people are like you, overworked and trampled by the demands of their life. But you don't have to be part of the crowd that hits the snooze button, breaks their resolutions, and delays their dreams. You can get what you want and you can achieve what you desire without blowing up your life. You must simply adopt a powerful mindset and push yourself to take action when you don't feel like it. To be powerful, you must make it happen while you worry that you can't. You must push yourself to do the things you don't want to do so that you can become the person you were meant to be.

Nothing is stopping you from achieving your goals, nothing but you and your dumb excuses. You can stay where you are or you can change your life. Of course, it takes effort, but it's not as hard as you believe. Don't be too timid and squeamish about your actions. You can't build a reputation based on what you're going to do.

All of life is an experiment.

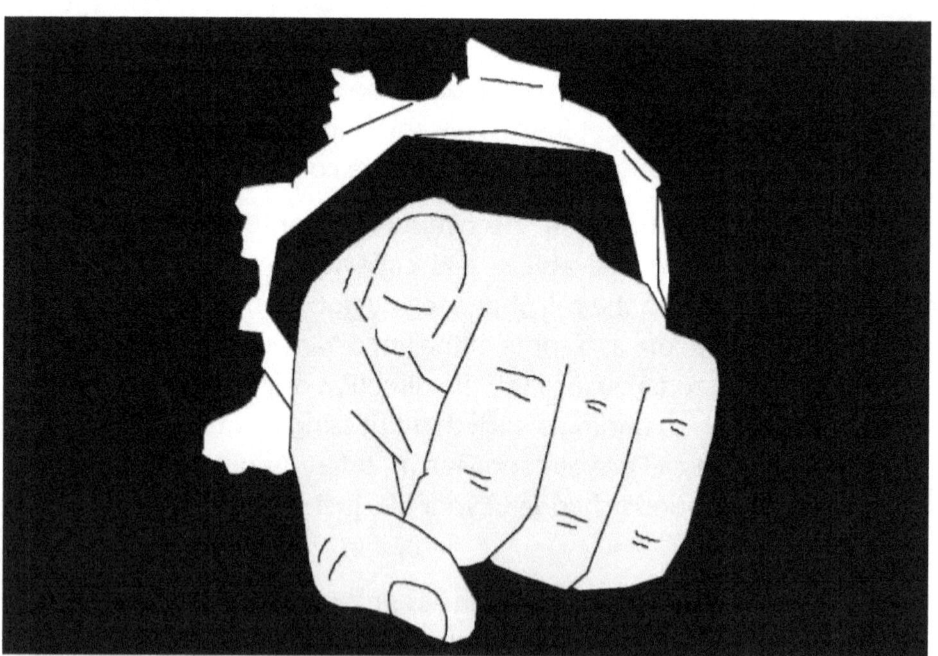

THE PROBLEM IS YOU

What is the biggest obstacle between you and the life you want? I'm sure money, time, experience, and circumstances come to mind. You are wrong. The biggest obstacle you face is you. You are in your way.

More precisely, it is your mindset.

You have adopted a rigid mindset that is preventing you from changing. A mindset is like a pair of sunglasses that filters all your thoughts and feelings. If you put on a pair of sunglasses with amber-coloured lenses, for example, it colours everything you see.

You get the idea! The sunglasses change what you see.

Your mindset changes how you think and feel. Depending on your mindset, your ideas either take flight or fizzle out into nothing. If you look at the world through a more powerful mindset, you can take on and accomplish anything.

The secret sauce is in solving the problem, not in not having problems in the first place. Taking responsibility for our problems is far more important because that is where real learning comes from.

'THE WIZARD'

A 15-year-old kid from America dreamed of becoming the greatest basketball player, but his dream was crushed when he was removed from the high school basketball team because he was not tall enough.

The team needed someone taller, so his close friend joined them. The boy's name was not on the list. He was embarrassed and devastated by this decision. He went home, closed the door, and cried for hours.

During the basketball season, he was so excited that he wanted to watch the other boys play. So he asked the coach if he could ride the bus with the team to the tournament. The coach agreed but under one condition. He told the boy that the sole way he could join them was to hold the player's uniforms. So that's what the boy did. He walked into the building carrying uniforms for the players who made fun of him.

He went to school early every day, arriving before everybody else did. He spent the morning practising shooting hoops in the gym. He was unstoppable in his desire to be the best in basketball, so much so that the physical education teachers had to drag him out of the gym when the bell for the first period rang.

The boy decided that nothing will stop him. He decided that failure and rejection won't discourage him and won't get in the way of his dream. Whenever he got tired and figured that he needed to stop, he would close his eyes and see the players' list without his name.

His diligence paid off when he made the team and instantly became their best player. He became one of the best basketball players of all time. He became a legend. His basketball career is fascinating and one of a kind. It includes 14 All-Star games and 2 Olympic gold medals. His NBA records are unbeatable. The kid is none other than Michael Jordan, one of the hardest-working athletes in the history of the sport.

'His Airness' was like a machine. He could do anything he wanted whenever he wanted on the hardwood.

Jordon, while embracing failure, uttered, "I've missed more than 9,000 shots in my career. I've lost almost 300 games. I've been trusted to take the game's winning shot twenty-six times and have missed. I've failed over and over and over again in my life. And that is why I succeed."

THE BIGGEST OBSTACLE TO LEARNING

What have you always struggled to learn?

Whether you're a poor writer or can't handle numbers, you're no different from everyone else.

You may have experienced frustrations with learning. If only more people knew that the first and most important step to solving these problems is surprisingly simple. When you struggle to learn, you often put it down to a lack of innate ability.

At some point, you've used explanations such as, "I'm just not good with numbers," as you told yourself at school while wrestling with a hard math problem.

This perspective frames our capacity to learn something outside our control when in reality it's influenced heavily by our own beliefs.

If learning is a journey from a place of knowing less to a place of knowing more, then trying to learn something when you don't believe you can do it is like trying to drive with the handbrake on. Unsurprisingly, the idea that you need to believe in your capability to succeed isn't new and often appears in children's stories.

MODERN LIFE MAKES YOU FEEL STUCK

A feeling of control is the foundation of human happiness. When you feel like there are too many things outside your control, you start feeling powerless and unhappy.

When you feel like your own actions can't make a true difference in the direction your life is taking, you start giving up. That's the precise moment that you become stuck.

There's something about life today that makes it easy to get stuck. The outside world operates on your inner well-being. Between the increasingly frantic pace of daily life, financial problems, and an endless stream of distractions, it is no wonder that you feel like you can't be your best. You are simply spending less time focusing on yourself.

When you're surrounded by change and you're constantly adapting to new conditions, it lowers your desire and ability to change. The world beneath your feet may change completely and this has an enormous impact on how you feel. The web has increased the amount of information you process every day explosively and has created the need to adapt to a constant series of new gadgets and ideas.

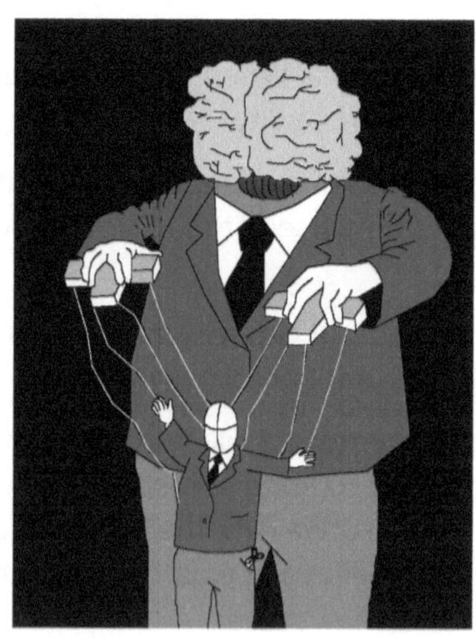

The ultimate effect of all this change on society is still unknown. The only thing that is not in dispute is the fact that there is a negative effect on your brain.

New problems and new decisions arrive at your doorstep each week. This may include deciding how much television or internet kids can watch or just trying to eat mindfully. You constantly feel that you are just barely keeping up.

The modern world teaches you that there are too many things out of your control. As if all these external factors weren't enough, your mind begins working against you too. As the world inserts all sorts of uncertainties into your life, your mind supplements them by casting doubts. When you feel stuck, you become acutely aware of what's missing in your life.

Your mind tries to figure out what's wrong, and focuses on the past, highlighting and even inventing a series of missteps. You are forced to make big decisions that impact the direction of your life. Some of these include the schools you attend, the jobs you accept, the monthly expenses you need to cover, the friends you keep, and maybe even marriage and children. These decisions stick with you for a long time.

As you look back at each decision and the path you took, you become more aware of the things you left behind. You twist these decisions, which were once powerful symbols of your achievements, into sacrifices. Instead of seeing what a new job brought into your life, you begin to think about all the other jobs it cut you off from.

To complete the issue, there doesn't seem to be any time to fix the problem. The demands of life can seem all-consuming. Sometimes it feels as if there is no time to move outside the daily routine and do something different.

After a long week, you look back and feel as if you had no spare time to do something interesting, just for yourself. What could you have possibly done to make a meaningful change if you can't spend time on yourself?

A lack of control inspires all sorts of negative habits. Without control, you start to question your place in life.

Some of these queries may include:

Where are you headed?

What is the point of it all?

Were your expectations too high?

Do you think your life is supposed to be unfulfilling?

THE SECRET TO SUCCESS

Once a young man asked Socrates about the secret of success. Socrates patiently listened to the man's question and told him to meet him near the river the next morning for the answer. The next morning Socrates asked the young man to walk with him towards the river till the water came up to their neck. To the young man's surprise, Socrates ducked him into the water.

The young man struggled to get out of the water, but Socrates was strong and kept him there until the boy started turning blue. Socrates then pulled the man's head out of the water. The young man gasped and took a deep breath of air.

Socrates asked, "What did you want the most when your head was in the water?"

The young man replied, "Air."

Socrates said, "That is the secret to success. When you want success as badly as you wanted the air while you were in the water, then you will get it. There is no other secret."

Desire, burning desire, is basic to achieving anything beyond the ordinary. A burning desire is the starting point of all accomplishments. Just like a small fire cannot give much heat, a weak desire cannot produce great results.

WHAT TO DO?

A diamond is a chunk of coal that did well under pressure. If you can reclaim control over 10 per cent of your life, and spend that time doing something productive, energy-inspiring, and action-oriented, you will quickly restore order and balance in your life. You will find all the routine, uncertainty, and difficulty significantly more tolerable. You will discover that this small 10 per cent acts like an anchor to reorient your whole perspective. Once you've achieved that small foothold, many things will fall back into place.

But brace yourself, that first 10 per cent is the hardest. No one builds a legacy by standing still.

Imagine a movie or story without any action. How boring it would be!

Action is the key to becoming more powerful. An action is a thought brought to life. Something as simple as getting up from your chair and stepping outside begins with a thought. Being stuck places a buffer between what you're thinking and what you can do about it. You're just a spectator. When you take action, your thoughts animate your mind.

Every action starts with an inner, mental impulse. Action is your bridge from the inside to the outside.

In life, 80% of the outcome is usually the result of 20% of your total effort. This is commonly called the Pareto Principle.[1]

The feeling of control is tightly linked to action. When you take action and see positive results in the world, you feel powerful. But when you feel that your actions don't make any difference in the world, or that it's hardly even worth taking the action, you feel hopeless and unhappy.

Something feels broken inside when you're stuck. Your mind is still working fine because you can imagine the way your life should be going perfectly. Your thoughts give you a very clear picture of the way things are supposed to be. You keep looking for ways to make a change. But something is preventing your deepest desires from translating into concrete action.

ELEMENTS OF LIFE

Every experience in every moment of your life contains two primary elements. One is the outside world—the setting and the circumstances that frame the moment. The other is the set of feelings, thoughts, and

---

1. https://www.briantracy.com/blog/personal-success/how-to-use-the-80-20-rule-pareto-principle/

attitudes within you that both drive and respond to the moment. When you feel as though you lack control over your life, it's because you feel that both parts are preventing you from taking meaningful action.

You're locked up as if both your inner and outer worlds are ganging up to keep you from moving forward. You must start by taking back control of your head if you want to gain control over your life.

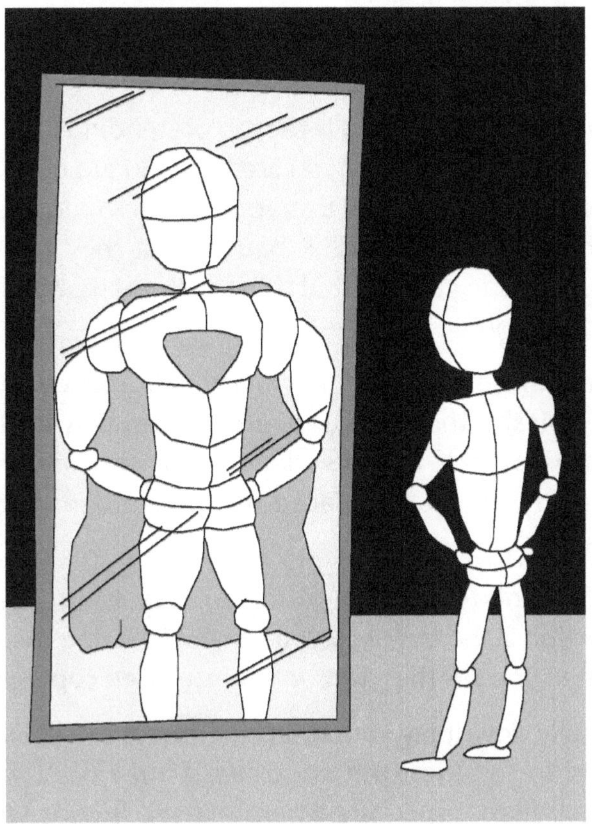

Don't package your dreams as a huge accomplishment or else you'll feel numb and never start. Push yourself into action by focusing on the steps in the process or by merely getting started. You will probably feel overwhelmed at first and intimidated by the size and scale of change that would be needed to make a true difference in your life. When you picture it like that, the change feels so enormous that only a mammoth or explosive effort could reach you there. It feels completely out of the question that you'll just drop a grenade into your life.

Without consciously and actively nurturing the kind of approach that lets you see something bigger for yourself while rebuilding the bridge between idea and action, you will continue to fall into the same traps as you've earlier.

IS EVERYTHING OKAY?

The first step to moving forward is to stop pretending that everything is okay. You must stop saying that you are fine. You are not fine. You need to quit pretending that you are. Everyone is stuck in some area of their lives, pretending that it is not that bad so that they can justify doing nothing. You persuade yourself that things are not that bad because you don't want to change.

You also minimise the situation when you don't know how to change something. Ironically, the more trapped you feel by your life, the more you'll convince yourself that it's okay. When you finally stop giving excuses and admit it, you'll be faced with the sobering reality of how much work is in front of you.

You don't want to tell the truth because lying to yourself and justifying inaction is the only way you can avoid facing the fear of taking a risk. As soon as you tell the truth, you shatter your coping mechanisms.

You normally downplay your disappointment in life. Everyone does. No one wants to tell the truth about what they want and how they feel about their lives, especially when you see friends with their cool lives on Instagram. The pressure to make sure that you are keeping up is everywhere. But keeping up with appearances won't help you take action. It's not powerful.

You cannot get what you want if you refuse to face the truth that you are struggling. You long for more. That tension between where you are now and what you want to become is what makes you human.

You've already proven that you're susceptible to hitting the snooze button and getting stuck. You know that you can undermine your goals.

WHO IS YOUR BEST FRIEND AND YOUR WORST ENEMY?

There's a battle going on in your brain and it's keeping you from getting what you want. To win any fight you have to know what you are up against and how to fight back.

Your brain is a formidable opponent and it fights dirty. At crucial moments throughout your day, your brain is putting the brakes on your desire for action and inserting thoughts and feelings to keep you from moving forward.

Yes, you read that right. You don't have the life that you want because your brain is keeping you from getting it. It pits your feelings against your dreams. It sets your worries against your ambitions. It stacks up your frustrations against your future. You need to learn how to fight back and win.

Your feelings and mindset are driving inaction and interrupting the natural course of energy from thought to action. They keep you spinning in circles without growing or changing.

THREE-LEVEL MIND MODEL
CONSCIOUS MIND

The conscious mind is defined as a part of the mind which is responsible for rationalising, paying attention, logical thinking, and reasoning. For example, if an individual is asked to add one plus one, it is the conscious mind which will work on the calculation and give the answer.

It is also known to control all our day-to-day activities voluntarily. It is called the gatekeeper of the human mind.

It also keeps track of and communicates with the outside world and inner self through receptive sensations, thoughts, speech, pictures, writing, and physical activities.

UNCONSCIOUS MIND

It defines all past events and memories, though at times they are inaccessible to you no matter how hard you try to bring things up. For example, the first word you've learned to say, or how it felt to be able to walk on your own.

THE SUBCONSCIOUS MIND

Do you remember when you tried to ride a bicycle for the first time? Can you count the number of repetitions necessary to perform a flawless dance? Have you ever tried to master a new musical instrument?

Most likely, the first attempt to synchronise a new set of complex actions is always difficult. Once you become more skilled, these movements start to require less conscious awareness until everything begins to flow naturally.

All these automatic movements are guided by one of the most powerful inner forces which drive human behaviour—the subconscious mind.

The subconscious mind is defined as the section of mind which is responsible for all the involuntary actions and accessible information which are being received in daily life. For example, the continuous processes of breathing, blood circulation, and heartbeat are known to be controlled by an individual's subconscious mind.

It also exhibits all the reactions and automatic actions you can become aware of if you think about them. For example, your ability to drive a car. Once you are skilled at it, you stop thinking about which gears to use, which pedals to press, or which mirror to look at, yet you can always become aware of what you did once you think about it.

WHERE DOES THE SUBCONSCIOUS MIND HIDE?

It's not common to hear about conscious and unconscious actions when you talk about the brain. Whether you like it or not, your ability to control thoughts, synchronise movements, or experience emotions depends on the depth of information processing.

THE POWER OF YOUR SUBCONSCIOUS MIND

People say that the marvellous power of your subconscious mind can bring you more power, wealth, health, happiness, and joy in your life. You can do this by learning to contact and release the hidden power of your subconscious mind.

A new light can inspire you and you can generate a new force enabling you to realise your hopes and make all your dreams come true. Decide to make your life grander, greater, richer, and nobler than ever!

The infinite intelligence within your subconscious mind can reveal everything you need to know at every moment and every point in time, provided you are open-minded and receptive.

You can receive new thoughts and ideas enabling you to bring forth new inventions, make discoveries, or write books and plays. Moreover, the infinite intelligence in your subconscious can bestow you with wonderful and original knowledge. It can reveal and open the way for perfect expression and a true place in your life.

It is your right to discover this inner world of thought, feeling, and power, of light, love, and beauty. Though invisible, its forces are mighty. Within your subconscious mind, you will find the solution for every problem, and the cause for every effect. Because you can draw out the hidden powers, you come into actual possession of the power and wisdom necessary to move forward in abundance, security, joy, and dominion.

People believe that there is a miraculous healing power in your subconscious that can heal the troubled mind and the broken heart. It can open the prison door of the mind and liberate you.

Your feelings are a way of taking tons of incoming data and delivering it to your conscious mind as a kind of fuzzy sentiment to steer your decisions.

Your unconscious mind may be less like a wizard behind the curtain and a lot more like a bunch of very fast processors all working together. They are just like traders in the stock market who are used to making many decisions very quickly.

Your conscious mind is creative. You cannot always control what happens to you. But you can always control how you interpret what happens to you as well as how you respond.

People who feel entitled view every occurrence in their life as either an affirmation of or a threat to their greatness. You need some sort of existential crisis to take an objective look at how you've been deriving your meaning in life and then can consider changing course.

YOUR ASPIRATIONS IN LIFE COME FROM YOUR CONSCIOUS MIND

The conscious mind is the creative one, it creates all of your desires, wishes, what you want to do with your life and more. Your conscious mind can learn easily from seeing people doing things, watching a movie, reading a book, cooking, or walking.

One day, you can watch some random guy replacing the keyboard of a tiny laptop and think to yourself, "You know what, I can do this too!"

Then you find yourself buying the tools, rolling up your sleeves, and changing the keyboard of your laptop. You may then decide to open a repair store for phones and laptops. The next day, you might maybe want to be a karate master after watching Bruce Lee's stunts.

YOUR SUBCONSCIOUS MIND IS THE HABIT MIND

When you receive a stimulus and there is a habit in the subconscious mind related to that stimulus, it will automatically engage in its related behaviour. That's what a habit is, all it takes is a stimulus and the behaviour will play itself out. When your conscious mind is lost in thinking, your subconscious mind automatically determines your behaviour.

This is why you don't need to stop cycling when you start thinking about what to cook when you arrive home. You can even go ahead and try to remember the recipe and figure out if you need to stop at the supermarket to get a missing ingredient while your subconscious mind does the crucial work for you i.e. get you home.

The conscious mind changes easily, whereas the subconscious mind is more stubborn. Thoughts come and go in your conscious mind. It constantly changes. Your subconscious mind takes a little bit more than that to be convinced about the changes you've been proposing. It won't change until you keep repeating the action forever.

Imagine a world in which your subconscious mind changes as quickly as your conscious mind does. God forbid, you may end up learning to walk every day.

MINDFULNESS

Being mindful is a way of life where you keep your conscious mind in the present moment and don't let it wander. If your conscious mind is in the present then it runs your behaviour. Naturally, it leaves lesser space for your subconscious to take the wheel.

If you manage to stay mindful sometimes every day and enforce your new 'changed' or 'modified' behaviours, then you can slowly but eventually, change your subconscious programmes. You can get closer to your subconscious mind through regular practice.

You've survived before, you will survive again. It is your subconscious mind that comes through to tell you, "You can do it," when faced with a challenging situation. As you live your life, your subconscious mind accumulates memories of times when you've succeeded and stores them for later use.

Even if you are in a hard situation that you've never been in before, your subconscious can push you on, because it remembers times when you have conquered a new obstacle. Your subconscious mind is that friend who whispers in your ear.

PUSHING THROUGH THE WALL

When you are feeling stuck, pushing through is the universal solution for dealing with it. There is no point wallowing in the reasons for the things that have slowed you down. No matter what is slowing you down—fear or anger—you need to figure out what is going to advance your personal goals and start taking action accordingly.

If you don't have what you want in one area of your life, defy your feelings and do what you must achieve it. Remember, all those feelings and doubts and concerns are nothing more than your brain's expression of the unknown.

Your doubts are not a true, objective gauge of how good you are at something. Your doubts are simply expressing your brain's concern that you haven't had a lot of practice with the skills required for the task at hand.

The key to getting yourself unstuck is to start saying yes to those unexpected impulses that want to take you somewhere new. These will not only relieve you of the monotony of life but also provide other benefits to your mind and your happiness.

SNOOZE - KEY TAKEAWAYS

1. You are constantly operating from one of two forces inside you. The powerful you versus the resistant you.

2. The powerful version of yourself loves discovery, curiosity, and challenges. It wants you to grow, move and expand. Resistance is the equal and opposite force that works to hold you back. At every moment, the choice is always yours and you decide who will lead your action.

3. Motivation is unreliable and based on our energy levels which change from time to time, day after day. They tend to domino. Each setback saps your energy further, making the next failure more likely.

4. Motivation is connected to emotions and feelings which fluctuate and change quickly and constantly. You cannot rely on what you cannot control.

5. You need an alternative energy source to propel you forward. Put your stock in determination.

6. Determination is the decision to take action and continue to do so despite forces pushing against it. Determination is not swayed by emotion but built by commitment, action, and habits.

7. You are stuck in your life and are pretending that it's not that bad so that you can justify doing nothing. The more trapped you feel by your life, the more you'll convince yourself it's okay.

8. The perfect signs of being 'stuck' include times when life begins to slow down, when you feel like doing nothing, and when everything slips away and you let it go.

9. Difficult times during life challenges can have you feeling like you've lost your sense of direction. You are probably circling the changes you want to make to your life but you might fail to realise that you're stuck in a loop.

10. The uncertainty of life in the twenty-first century has a big impact on your ability and capacity to change. Certainty is the rival of growth.

11. The biggest obstacle you face is you. The obstacle between you and the life you want is your rigid mindset.

12. The world is undergoing radical changes at an accelerated speed. Innovation, digitalisation, and technological progress have fundamentally changed and have had an enormous impact on how you feel.

13. The feeling of control is the foundation of human happiness. Reclaim control over 10 per cent of your life by spending that time doing something productive, energy-inspiring, and action-oriented. You will quickly restore order and balance to your life.

14. Your feelings and rigid mindset are driving your inaction and interrupting the natural course of energy from thought to action, keeping you spinning in circles without growing or changing.

15. Desire, burning desire, is basic to achieving anything beyond the ordinary.

16. You are so preoccupied with your belief systems that you are heading toward self-destruction. You have no idea how much easier things could be if you stopped being so hard on yourself.

17. Your mind will trick you into expending enormous amounts of energy by keeping you stuck. By stewing over what-ifs, you're taking time and energy away from more productive pursuits.

18. The pressure to make sure that you are keeping up is everywhere. But keeping up with appearances won't help you take action. It's not powerful.

19. New things don't feel safe. They make the forecasting engine in your mind go haywire. The only thing that makes you feel safe is what you already know—being stuck.

20. The only thing to do when the what-ifs come is to push through. Being powerful doesn't mean the what-ifs disappear, it means you ignore them and move forward.

21. You cannot get what you want if you refuse to face the truth. You are struggling. You long for more. You are not alone. That tension between where you are now and what you want to become is what makes you human.

22. Whether you're eleven years old or forty, when you start worrying, it doesn't mean anything will go wrong. It just means you are about to try something new.

23. Pushing yourself to take simple actions creates a chain reaction in your confidence and your productivity. If you don't learn how to untangle your feelings from your actions, you'll never unlock your true potential.

24. When it comes to your dreams, you have two choices: pursue them or be haunted by them. You are one decision away from a completely different life. Win or lose, at least start doing something.

25. The snooze button is the perfect symbol of human resistance and the emblem of anyone who feels stuck.

CHAPTER-2

ROUTINE

You would be the weirdest alien on this planet if you don't do anything by routine. These days everyone feels a bit blah or bored or burned by life. The majority of people can't stand their jobs. They are getting older every year, working more, and sleeping less and their overall happiness is declining.

Anytime you start feeling overloaded with choices, overwhelmed with uncertainty, or locked into an inescapable routine, you become stuck.

TOO MANY CHOICES

You live in a society where you can have pretty much anything. And that's the way it should be. You believe that freedom translates into the power of choice. You can choose what you watch, what you hear, what you do, and what you think. But something happened along the way.

The power of choice has exploded into something overpowering that undermines your mental well-being. A quick trip down any supermarket aisle will demonstrate the problem. Why do we need to decide between thirty types of rice, hundreds of different cereals, and dozens of chocolate?

There are plenty of economists who could explain why choice is important and how it increases competition and diversity. When you have too many choices, no matter what you decide, you will think about all the options you left behind. Even if you were happy with your choice, the knowledge that you could have chosen differently makes you start to wonder if you missed out by not choosing something else. When you think about what to do with your life, this can be paralysing. That's the paradox. Your life always expresses the result of your dominant thoughts and the choices you make.

UNCERTAINTY

In this fast-moving world, an important reason for getting stuck is the increased level of uncertainty in your life. Uncertainty keeps you from trying new things, moving faster, or even moving at all. When you feel uncertain, you become stuck.

You all find yourselves faced with uncertainty. There's no way to peer into the future to see what it holds. Uncertainty is a part of the human experience. Uncertainty is all around you, never more so than today. Much of what lies ahead in life remains uncertain, whether it concerns a global pandemic, the economy, or your finances, health, and relationships.

Yet, as human beings, you crave security. You want to feel safe and have a sense of control over your lives and well-being. Fear and uncertainty can leave you feeling stressed, anxious, and powerless over the direction of your life. It can drain you emotionally and trap you in a downward spiral of endless 'what-ifs' and worse-case scenarios about what tomorrow may bring.

You are all different in how much uncertainty you can tolerate in life. When it strikes, there is no way to predict what will happen if you take a risk. However, there is indeed no way to predict what will happen if you don't take a risk either. The idea that staying stuck is keeping you safe is an illusion. No matter what you do, life will surprise you.

The difference is that when you make a positive change by adopting a growth mindset, you are choosing to take on the uncertainty of life on your terms. The mistake is thinking that there is an antidote to uncertainty.

LESS ROUTINE MORE LIFE

The biggest reason you are so stuck is that you are used to it. Modern life throws so many choices and so much uncertainty at you that it feels like the only way to cope is by spending all of your energy keeping your life in a comfortable routine, even though it's not making you happy.

You instinctively value familiarity over the risk of change and unsurprisingly, you become dissatisfied. When you're locked into a routine, nothing exciting seems to be heading your way. It's just the same old boring stuff, day in and day out. But as much as you may want a change, the truth is that you feel comfortable in your routine, even if it isn't making you happy.

You wake up at the same time, brush your teeth, dress generally in the same style, eat largely the same breakfast, fix your coffee in a specific way, commute to work the same way, and so on.

Obviously, routines are a requirement in daily life, but they're a devil's bargain. They automate your brains, structure your lives, and make things easier, but in return, they rob your day of variety and creativity. They erase any sense of exploration. There's nothing that can make you feel quite as robotic as a routine.

When you're stuck, you've taken this too far. You channel yourself into a routine that submerges any sense of difference between the days. You may arrive at work and don't quite remember getting yourself there. Taking the same path to work every day creates a 'stable environment' that promotes automated thinking.

That kind of routine can be as hard to shake as a cigarette addiction. You want to quit the habit but there are too many situational cues and the path in your mind is well-worn and just too difficult to move out of. In the case of addiction, you see a cigarette and you feel an immediate compulsion to smoke because you know from a whole series of past actions that smoking a cigarette delivers the nicotine buzz. Your brain has already built a direct shortcut from trigger to reward. The strength of these compulsions can be very hard to fight. Routine is like an addiction to your daily life from which you can't break free. Your brain keeps clicking back into old modes, trigger to reward, sparked by the repetition of all the cues you experience every day.

TAKE THE RISK OR LOSE THE CHANGE

Your life is waiting to expand into something much larger and the only thing holding you back is your brain. You'll never feel like doing what you must do. Being powerful means being willing to be uncomfortable. You must be willing to fall. Whenever you find yourself overwhelmed with fear or clinging rigidly to what you know to avoid any kind of risk, that is a signal to take action.

What you've done instead is listened to an infinite variety of persuasive arguments that your brain makes to convince you to not take action. When the time comes to lean towards what you want, you do nothing and it will let you have nothing.

To recognise these moments as a signal to act and to trust them while doing the opposite of what you 'feel' like isn't easy.

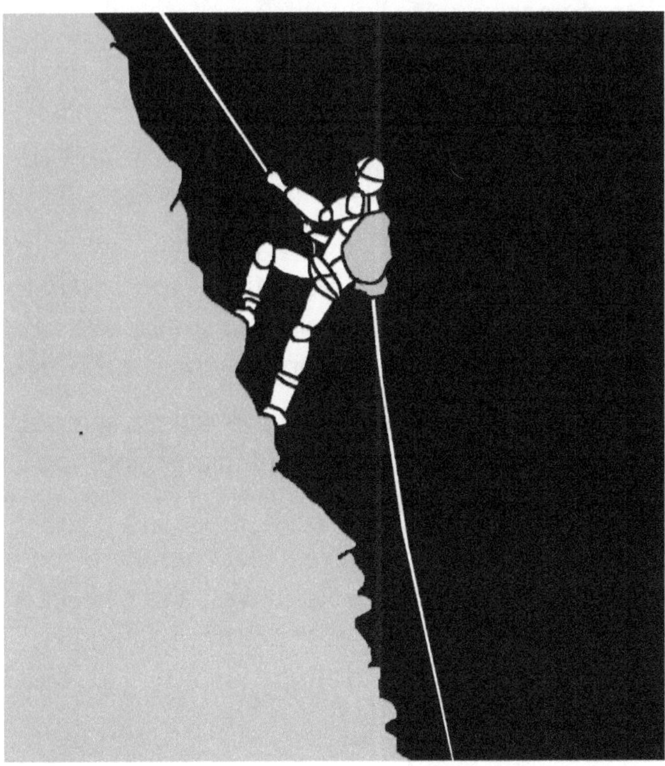

Learning to lean into things that make you uncomfortable takes practice. You are about to learn a method that will train you to build momentum in your life and become an expert at taking action. Trying to be happy when you aren't or making do with what you have or waiting for the right time to make your big move will not give you what you want. If you are addicted to your comfort zone, and only do what feels easy, you will never get what you want.

I suppose people on their deathbeds don't want to look back at their life and regret all the things they didn't do. Nobody wants to say that his or her life was just 'okay.' But if you don't start doing what feels hard, that is exactly what will happen. Choosing the path of least resistance is the core reason why your life isn't going anywhere. You're making hundreds of small decisions each day to stay exactly where you are.

Not talking about improving your skillset is a decision. Skipping the gym every day is a decision. Not coming out of your comfort zone is a decision. Not exploring new career opportunities is a decision. Not taking a risk to change your life is a decision.

The human behaviour of taking the easy path actually makes no sense. By chasing easy pleasures, you lose happiness. Doing passive activities such as scrolling social media or leisure time or always binge-watching Netflix makes you less productive compared to doing something active.

What are you getting from doing nothing? Not much. In fact, after about thirty minutes of passive activity, you'll start to zone out completely. It's that mental zone where you completely check out and do nothing. Your mind has stopped doing anything useful or productive.

So why do you do it? Simple! You have trained yourself to hit the snooze button. If there's a way to avoid doing anything, you'll do it, even though it won't make you productive.

Change means risk. Maybe you feel like your life is too fragile. You can't afford to break anything, so you hold on and protect what you've got. Doing nothing feels like the best bet from all angles. That might make sense if you were a robot and all you knew was routine. But there's a lot more going on as a human.

Your imagination is designed to come up with game-changing ideas for a reason. Your imagination is designed to push you in new directions and help you grow. You need to honour your creativity and inventiveness by delivering change through action.

ADMIT IT!

Admitting to yourself, let alone to others, that you're stuck can feel monumentally difficult. Just like most secrets you keep, you feel ashamed and hate confronting your imperfections.

Once you begin facing the truth that you feel stuck, the natural conclusion is that you've done something wrong. When you're stuck, you experience disappointment and frustration daily. It could be the humiliation of doing work that lowers your intelligence level and your creativity or having to drag around a body that's a walking indictment of your bad eating and exercise habits or the lonely regret of knowing that you've squandered too many years away without chasing your dreams. You feel like your life is empty of purpose.

It's never going to make you a bad person. Under the circumstances, that kind of denial may be very appropriate if you've got a big road to climb to get your life back on track.

But feeling miserable all the time is not sustainable. If you don't accept, you won't attempt to change and if you don't change you won't progress. That's a fixed mindset. There's no way you can confront and solve all your problems at once.

BE HAPPY, IT DRIVES PEOPLE CRAZY!

You deny how you feel because, in our society, you're not supposed to be unhappy. There are all sorts of explicit and unspoken reasons for this. You know about the relentless chorus of positive thinkers who claim that just thinking happy thoughts will change your life. They are wishful thinkers who believe that by transforming your thoughts, you will magically transform your life. Most people would hate to monitor their thoughts for signs of unhappiness like an air traffic controller.

Leaving aside the so-called magnetic frequencies of your thoughts and the harmful radiation that emanates from negative thoughts, I think a more plausible explanation for hiding your unhappiness is that you sense it's a social liability. People like to hear about your problems only to the degree that it makes them feel better.

The problems that come from feeling stuck are repetitive and boring and they will seem fairly uninteresting to others, especially if you aren't doing anything about them. Unless you are actively attacking your problems and impressing your friends through your efforts to fix things, your frequent conversations about feeling stuck may let your friend think that you are a social downer. So you start expressing your views on 'Game of thrones.'

This creates social pressure to put on a happy face and talk about all the things that are going well in your life. But even though it might not make you the world's most popular person in the short term, if you don't talk about what's wrong, you are not merely misleading others, you're also misleading yourself. I'm not saying you need to send out weekly newsletters to everyone expressing how you feel, but it is essential to find some vehicle for confronting how you feel. If you're lucky enough to have an ally you can trust, that's great.

DENIAL AIN'T JUST A RIVER IN EGYPT

Just as keeping quiet about your problems is a form of denial, you're creating a Cinderella mythology for yourself with the secret hope that a fairy will rescue you.

The simple truth is that no one is coming to save you. No one is going to jump into your life and radically change its direction. It's also true that no one can stop you from trying to soldier through your life. You will be better off if you focus less on your existential stamina and your ability to endure an unfulfilling situation and more on discovering and striving for what you want.

Even without the social code of always needing to appear happy, you feel ashamed to expose yourself. You all know the cliched reasons for wanting to hide the truth, like the embarrassment and frustration of working a job that you hate, the isolation of fighting a health problem, or the secret behind your weight problem. But another major reason for not admitting that you're stuck is that you expose your mistakes.

When you have a problem that you can't get past, there probably is some sort of character fault. But who the hell doesn't have one? You can't simply get comfortable with the idea of your imperfections. Maybe you are a bit argumentative, selfish, greedy, or mostly lazy. Big deal! You are avoiding acceptance because you feel that it will reflect badly on your abilities or talents or character. But you are just continuing the problem that keeps you stuck.

Put yourself on the line, and you can start fixing your problems and getting what you want.

CONFESS WHAT YOU TRULY WANT

Confessing your true desires can be traumatic for people for a variety of reasons. Sometimes because it's so completely out of character, goes against the grain of your social circle, or is just plain expensive. You may even need a lot of pills to gather the courage.

Admitting and stating what you want clearly and confidently can be tough because that may involve confronting what might be a huge gap between reality and fantasy. The dreams that you harbour about how your life can be sometimes sound pretty far-fetched. You may feel as if your goal is so impossibly far away that you would rather not talk about it. You feel that it sounds ridiculous to talk about something that might take years to achieve and will take a tremendous amount of work.

Facing the truth is tough. No one wants to collapse on the bed and sob over the state of their life. It's so much easier to stay busy, think about something else, insist that it's fine, and wait for the day when your mindset will magically change and altering your life will seem easy. But that day is not coming.

You will never just wake up with the motivation and fortitude that you've been missing for years. Your brain does not work that way. The only choice you have is to force yourself to change whether you feel like it or not because when you postpone the moment for action, your resistance wins. The first step to killing resistance and taking action is to tell the truth.

Your deepest desires are the most important tools you have to help you push through resistance. It's time to use them. Your desire acts like a honing device. If you tune into it, it will point you in the direction you are meant to go. Admitting what you want is the way to harness your desires and develop momentum. This might sound obvious and simple, but it's not. To admit what you want can be embarrassing. It can seem like a cliché or patently impossible. The idea that you might not get what you want can be so terrifying that you avoid admitting your wants. Or maybe you don't know what you want. You just know you're not happy with what you have. If you admit it, you will instantly give your life some direction. You will feel less afraid, which will make it easier to avoid taking the easy choice. In imagining your future, you will start to build it.

INATTENTIONAL BLINDNESS
INVISIBLE GORILLA TEST

In an experiment, researchers asked participants to watch a video of people tossing a basketball, and the observers were told to count the number of passes or to keep track of the number of throws versus bounce passes. Afterwards, the participants were asked if they had noticed anything unusual while watching the video. Across all the tests, approximately 50% of the participants reported seeing nothing out of the ordinary.

But in reality, something odd had happened. In some instances, a woman dressed in a gorilla suit strolled through the scene, turned to the camera, thumped her chest, and walked away. While it may seem impossible that the participants missed such a sight, their attention was focused elsewhere and on a demanding task, hence the gorilla became invisible.

You miss an enormous number of opportunities to change your life daily because you are not focused on what you want. You are focused on your problems and maintaining the illusion that you are fine. Unless and until you face the truth about your life and start focusing on opportunities to take action, you will continue to miss the gorilla moonwalking in your life.

YOU ARE CRAFTING NARRATIVES THAT KEEP YOU STUCK

Admitting what you truly want can be extremely tough for some people. That's because most of you tell yourselves that you can't have what you want or don't deserve it.

There are few things that human beings find more compelling than a story. You use stories not just for entertainment, but to make sense of the world and your place in it. You turn your lives into narratives and cast yourselves as heroes.

This might not sound problematic, but consider that when you turn yourself into a hero and build a fairy tale, it allows you to reinterpret everything wrong with your life in a way that makes it seem fine, admirable, or outside of your control.

CONNECTIONS

Your relationship with people is the most important aspect of your life. Communicating is one of the most productive forms of action you can take. Every time you share your ideas or ask for someone's help, you're learning subtle new skills about yourself and others. At the same time, you're advancing your agenda and taking concrete steps toward your goals.

Ask anyone who went through medical school and he or she will tell you that you can't learn how to truly land on your feet without sparring with a partner. Preparedness and memorisation count, but there's something else you learn when you rely on your verbal skills and perform a mock trial.

That's because plain old thinking relies on a well-worn, overused bookish system. Your schooling has made you proficient at memorising and juggling ideas in your minds. Thinking is not hard. It's when you're forced to socialise, persuasively convey meaning, and juggle facts and rhetoric that your brains are challenged and you discover what you're capable of. It's a skill that must be acquired.

ZOOM OUT

You live at a time unlike any other. Your grandparents and your parents did not have the tools that you have at your disposal. If they wanted to change their lives, it took a lot of money, a new degree, and probably moving several hundred kilometres. In practice, most of them didn't have a chance in hell of changing anything. They were stuck in the same job, the same circle of friends, and the same town for most of their adult lives. The only thing that changed was the seasons.

But the world has changed enormously since then. Unlike your parents, you have exactly what you need to get what you desire. Because of technology, the proliferation of information on the web, hyperconnectivity, and oversharing through social media, you have access to everything you need.

There's a way to get whatever you want without requiring money, a degree, or a move across the country. And no matter how crazy, far-fetched, or scary your desire feels, there is someone on the planet who has done it and has probably blogged about it, been featured in some magazine, or joined an online group to get it done. There is a living, breathing example of the life you imagine out there right now, and you are going to use that person and all the tools at your disposal to help yourself get that life.

YOU NEED A MAP

Maybe until now, you've been wandering through your life without any real direction. You're like a stubborn driver lost on back roads in a place you don't know. You have no idea where you are, so you obsessively focus on what is right in front of you. There are signs on all the roads, but you have no context to know which ones are right. So you take whichever turn 'feels' right, hoping to somehow find your path based on luck and gut feeling alone. Of course, most of the time that just leaves you even more lost. Just like any stuck driver, the only way you're ever going to get where you want to be is if you use a map and zoom out to get some perspective on where you stand in relation to the life you want.

Think of a program like Google Maps. You input where you are, and where you want to be and suddenly you not only have a map but a much larger perspective on where your journey fits into the world. You can zoom in to examine important details or zoom out for the big picture. Anytime you get lost on your trip, you can just glance down at the map and see how to keep moving in the right direction.

You might not know it, but you can do the same thing with your own life. ShareGPT won't do it for you, but that's okay because it isn't hard. The thing to remember is that somewhere out there, what you desire exists, so you need to figure out where you stand in relation to it. Seeing the gap will help you understand how to close it. Until now, you haven't been able to see a way to get what you desire. You need a map to help you break down the path between where you are right now and where you want to be. If you don't have a map, even if you're fully committed to change, chances are you will get lost. Your map will look like an aerial view of a river with a lot of rocks. You are on one side and what you want is on the other. Your job is to jump across all the rocks to get to the other side.

Every rock in the river represents an action—a person to reach out to, a meeting to attend, a business plan to write, a task you must complete, classes to take, research to do, a website to build, training to get, and conversations you must have.

USE AN EXPLORER'S PHILOSOPHY

Your map is not a step-by-step set of directions. It is a tool for giving you the perspective you need to creatively get what you want. The problem with directions like that is they are too rigid. What if you miss a turn? What if there's construction, and one of the roads you were told to take is blocked off? If all you have are a rigid set of step-by-step instructions, the moment you hit an unexpected snag or make a single mistake, you'll be lost.

Your dreams are like a massive road trip. If you tried to plot every single turn and road you should take, you will inevitably get lost. You will hit some obstacle along the way like an accident or traffic or some confusing signs and all of a sudden your carefully plotted directions would be useless. A good map allows you to adapt to whatever obstacles you hit and keep moving. If you're getting bored of the interstate, change the route along the way. The options are endless when you have a map to guide you.

The same is true about the path of life. Things never happen in the order you plan. Instead, when you start rolling and weird things happen, coincidences appear, and opportunities come out of nowhere. You want that to happen!

THIS IS A CREATIVE EXERCISE

You must expand your thinking here, not shrink it. To make your map, just list the things you need to do. When you find yourself knocking things off the list, you are shrinking your thinking. Stop that!

Everything that you should do and that comes to mind goes on the map. Along with this, anything remotely related to this thing you desire will be placed on the map. A map doesn't come with a timeline or a clock, so don't worry about how long things might take or when you might find the time to do them. But if it needs to happen at some point fix the deadline and write it down.

EXPLORING YOUR FULL POTENTIAL

Once your categories are defined, begin writing your thoughts freely along with feelings or observations about each.

To spark ideas, ask yourself:

- What's most important to you about this part of your life and why?

- What would success ideally look like to you?

- What's the one thing you would change if you could?

KEEPING YOUR GOALS IN MIND ALL YEAR

The last thing you want to do is create an amazing set of well-defined, achievable goals that would improve your life and then forget about it for the rest of the year. Once you have defined your goals, it's time to act on them.

LEAN INTO CHANGE

So now you have your map to guide you and keep you moving in the right direction. You know exactly what you have to do. But chances are when you sit down to do it, resistance will rear its ugly head again and you will soon feel paralysis kicking in. Your mind will start playing tricks on you. With your path all laid out in front of you, you will go into a hyperdrive of uncertainty. You will convince yourself that you don't have a clue about what to do first.

If you aren't empowered immediately and take action, you will chicken out of the whole thing or be a bit annoyed that it is going to be so much work. If you don't push through, you will soon be trapped inside your head with multiple queries such as those given below.

- Why am I doing this?
- Am I good enough to be doing this?
- Shouldn't I be doing something else?
- Isn't someone going to get mad about me doing this?
- I don't have the time to do this, am I kidding?

This is the moment. You will either stay stuck or you will push through. You must remember that there are no right moves. You can pick anything on your map to do right now and it will be a step forward.

Just remember that every single circle on your map takes you one step closer to what you desire. Every time you find yourself overanalysing your choices, stop yourself, pick anything on your map, and push through.

ACTIVATION ENERGY

To get what you want you must form an instant connection between what you want to do and doing it. The speed of that connection is critical to your success.

Activation energy is the amount of force required to take that first step. To create a new habit or action, the amount of force required is enormous. The longer you wait, the more you think, lower will be the impulse to take action. It loses its energy very quickly. Think about the force needed to take action or to get you to walk out of the door and exercise instead of hitting the snooze button. You prefer the snooze button because it takes too much activation energy to force yourself out of the door.

Taking action that fast will feel like the wrong thing to do. But that's just your resistance talking, begging you to hit snooze again. Remember, this is about decisions that are on your map, which means that, by definition, they are going to help you move toward your desire. Overanalysing them isn't going to do anything for you. The only wrong choice is to do nothing. If you push through, you will succeed. If you do nothing, you will get nothing. Any move you pick will push you toward what you want but finding the activation energy to make that move can be enormously difficult. So how, in that moment of fear, regret, panic, and longing do you force yourself to make a move?

ROUTINE - KEY TAKEAWAYS

1. The secret of your future is hidden in your daily routine. Breaking out of a routine creates a 'butterfly effect' in your life. You change one little thing about your day and it can set off an entire chain reaction.

2. Every new element that you introduce into your life becomes a clue to help you create a new direction. Every new direction is a pivotal point in your life and a lever against inertia.

3. Too many choices can overwhelm you and cause you to not choose at all. A plethora of choices makes it all the more difficult to make the best choice and you suffer from a choice overload.

4. Life is uncertain. Eat dessert first. The only way to make sense of change is to plunge into it, move with it, and join the dance.

5. You're stuck in life by living a comfortable routine. If you're a prisoner of routine, nothing exciting is heading your way and your captivity is eternal.

6. To regain control over your life you must stop pretending that everything is fine. Your brain works hard to insulate you but you've to face the fact that your life has not turned out as you had hoped.

7. Convincing yourself that you are fine is a great strategy for keeping yourself stuck.

8. Admit your wants. If you do, you will instantly give your life some direction and a beacon to be kept in sight. You will feel less afraid, which will make it easier to avoid making the easy choice.

9. You must be willing to fall. Whenever you find yourself overwhelmed with fear and clinging rigidly to what you know to avoid any kind of risk, that is a signal to take action.

10. If you don't accept, you won't attempt to change. If you won't change you won't progress. That's a fixed mindset. You can change your life just by paying attention to what's hidden inside your routines.

11. Slow down your routines and take them apart. Discover your own 'banner blindness.' You will end up finding small, positive things in your everyday patterns and can build on them. Less routine, more life.

12. The world is constantly telling you that the path to a better life is more. You are constantly bombarded by messages to pay attention. It's a social liability.

13. Keeping quiet about your problems is a form of denial. You're creating a Cinderella story for yourself, with the secret hope that a fairy will rescue you.

14. Comfort is an impermanent state of mind that humans love to call home. There's a certain comfort that comes from knowing how you fit in the world. Anything that shakes up that comfort potentially makes your life better, even if it is inherently scary.

15. Your deepest desires are tools that help you push through resistance. It's time to use them. Your desire acts like a honing device. If you tune into it, it will point you in the direction you are meant to go.

16. Your thoughts will spin off into endless circles and your life will go nowhere. But this is all just noise. Either stay stuck or push through.

17. Create your map to help guide you. Your mind will try to trick you. With your path all laid out in front of you, you will go into a hyperdrive of uncertainty. It is a sign to just keep going.

18. The values that you prioritise above everything else influence your decision-making more than anything else.

19. You miss an enormous number of opportunities to change your life daily because you are not focused on what you want.

20. People hate to monitor their thoughts for signs of unhappiness like an air traffic controller. Social pressure to put on a happy face are misleading. Indeed there has never been any explanation for the ebb and flow of happiness and unhappiness in our veins.

21. When you turn yourself into a hero and build a fairy tale, it allows you to reinterpret everything wrong with your life in a way that makes it seem fine, admirable, or outside of your control.

22. Never give yourself too much time. Work expands to fill the time available to complete it. If you're into productivity, you'll know this proverb as Parkinson's Law.

23. Once you have defined your goals, it's time to act on them. The last thing you want to do is create an amazing set of well-defined, achievable goals that would improve your life, and then forget about it for the rest of the year.

24. Activation energy is the initial push we require to take the first step. Your mind is very quick on killing any ideas, which requires you to move out of your comfort zone.

25. Activation energy in the moment of fear, regret, panic, and longing forces you to make a move and expresses your determination.

CHAPTER - 3

MINDSET

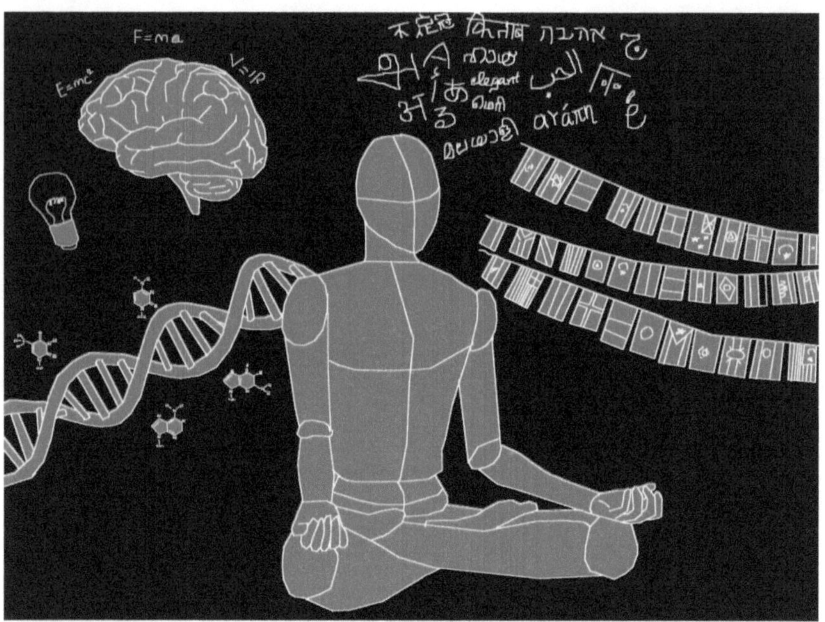

Mindset shapes the life you lead, the actions you take, and the future possibilities of the world you live in.

So what is a mindset? Do all people have a mindset? Does having a mindset matter?

Mindsets are assumptions that people use to make sense of the world. Each mindset is a belief about the world or human nature that isn't explicitly stated. People believe human qualities are carved in stone. If you succeed and avoid failures at all costs, you are smart. Failure means you aren't. It is that simple.

Struggles, mistakes, and perseverance are just not part of this picture. If human qualities are things that cannot be cultivated and are carved in stone, then why bother 'trying'?

Well, this is the reason why mindset exists.

Do the beliefs you have determine your mindset? Is your intelligence fixed? Is your personality fixed? Is your capability fixed? Is it possible to develop something that is fixed? What is the consequence of thinking that you can develop a trait as opposed to something fixed and deep-seated?

DO MINDSETS MATTER?

So why should you care about these complicated, nuanced assumptions about the world? Will it affect your success?

Your mindset affects the way you interpret events and your interpretation influences how you respond. People in the same situation could react very differently based on their mindset.

Mindset can determine whether you become the person you want to be and whether you accomplish the things you value.

How does this happen? How can a simple belief have the power to transform your life?

Believing that your qualities are carved in stone creates an urgency to prove yourself over and over again. If you have a limited amount of intelligence, personality, and moral character, then there is augmented pressure to prove that you have a healthy dose of these qualities. Some of us are trained in this mindset from an early age.

If you possess a better mindset and believe that you can be anything, then can you become the next Einstein or Beethoven?

WHY DO MINDSETS MATTER?

Mindsets shape the way you view the world. This simple belief can restrict or expand how you engage with life. Your mindset grows out of the experiences you have. Irrespective of whether the experience is positive or negative, a filter is formed that limits what your mind absorbs. This protects you and makes you feel secure in an uncertain world.

Paradoxically, by avoiding making mistakes and getting hurt, you quite unintentionally miss opportunities. You can even miss out on greater things by being fixed on replicating previous successes. You are usually totally unaware of all this.

Your mindset is normally in the background. To engage more fully you need to bring your mindset to the foreground. This requires a combination of specific experiences and reflections that enable you to become aware and then shift your mindset.

Your mindset plays a critical role in how you cope with life's challenges. It becomes a tool for greater achievement and increased effort. While facing a problem, people with better mindsets show greater resilience and they are more likely to persevere in the face of setbacks. If you have a fixed mindset, you are more liable to give up.

DO PEOPLE DIFFER?

You may have noticed that there are many similarities between humans and other animals. Both humans and animals eat, sleep, think, and communicate.

Are there any unique differences that set humans apart from all other animals?

All humans are born with the same physical features unless affected by a congenital disorder. These physical traits are fixed and are hard-wired into the genetic makeup. This is a result of selective evolution.

Do you differ if you have a different personality? Do each one of you represent a unique mix of different personality traits? If all are the same, then why is everyone not born with the same personality?

You differ in so many ways—your genetic make-up, sociocultural behaviour, attitudes, and in the way you speak listen, learn, behave, act, react and live.

Your experience and mindset make up your personality. Since the dawn of time, people have thought differently, acted differently, and fared differently from each other.

LIFE WITHOUT LIMBS

A child called Nick from Melbourne, Australia was born with an extremely rare congenital disorder known as phocomelia, which is characterised by the absence of legs and arms. While growing up, Nick struggled mentally, emotionally, and physically. He was bullied at school and attempted suicide when he was just 10 years old.

Arnold, an old janitor at his school was the first person who wanted the boy to become a speaker. But Nick opposed his idea as he was not confident. He was nervous and afraid to speak in front of an audience. But the janitor did not give up and relentlessly pursued the boy to share his life story. He chased Nick continuously for three months but the boy wouldn't agree until one day the janitor twisted his arm.

Nick gave his first speech when he was 19 and has never looked back. At that moment, he had found his purpose in life—to motivate people and inspire them to live amidst life's challenges. The boy is none other than Nick Vujicic, a world-renowned speaker.

Nick inherited his strong will from his mother. In one of his books, Nick said that her words set the tone for a lifetime.

"Nicholas," she said, "you need to play with normal children because you are normal. You just have a few bits and pieces missing, that's all."

PERCEPTION PRECEDES REALITY

The way you view life is not going to match with anyone else. Sure, you may have some moments where you and your friend perceive the same thing, but for the most part, you will see things slightly differently than your friend. Perception accounts for how you experience things as well as how you think and feel.

DO PERCEPTIONS LET US THINK?

In 1980, in a small village, a teacher teaching math to six-year-old Brian asked him, "If I give you one apple and one apple and one apple, how many apples will you have?"

Within a few seconds, Brian replied confidently, "Four!"

The dismayed teacher was expecting an effortless, "Three," the correct answer.

She was disappointed.

"Maybe the child did not listen properly," she thought.

She repeated, "Brian, listen carefully. It is very simple. You will be able to do it right if you listen carefully. If I give you one apple and one apple and one apple, how many apples will you have?"

Brian calculated again on his fingers. But within him, he was also searching for the answer that will make his teacher happy.

This time, hesitatingly, he replied, "Four."

The disappointment stayed on the teacher's face. Then she remembered that Brian loved strawberries. She thought that maybe he doesn't like apples and that is making him lose focus.

This time with exaggerated excitement and twinkling eyes she asked, "If I give you one strawberry and one strawberry and one strawberry, then how many will Brian have?"

Seeing the teacher happy, young Brian calculated on his fingers again. The teacher wanted her new approach to succeed.

With a hesitating smile, young Brian inquired, "Three?"

The teacher now had a victorious smile. Her approach had succeeded. She wanted to congratulate herself. But one last thing remained.

Once again she asked him, "Now if I give you one apple and one apple and one more apple, how many will you have?"

Brian answered, "Four."

The teacher was aghast.

"How Brian, how?" demanded the teacher, in a stern and irritated voice.

In a voice that was low and hesitating, young Brian replied, "Because I already have one apple in my bag."

Do you see the angle that everyone fails to see? If someone gives you an answer that is different from what you are expecting, is it necessarily wrong? Do you need to learn to appreciate and understand different perspectives? Do you impose your perspectives on others and then wonder what went wrong? Did the year in which the story happened matter? Does perception play the piano in what makes a person unique?

YOU ARE WHAT YOU BELIEVE YOURSELF TO BE!

Belief is another aspect that doesn't require introspection. Your experiences and perceptions in life create your beliefs. What you believe is what you perceive to be true based on what you have experienced in life. Your beliefs about yourself, other people, the world, what's right and wrong and everything else is never in a million years going to match exactly with someone else's beliefs.

THE ELEPHANT'S ROPE

Once, a man passing by saw a few domesticated elephants and stopped suddenly. He was confused by the fact that these huge creatures were being held by only a small rope tied to their front leg, with no chains or cages. It was obvious that the elephants could, at any time, break away from their bonds but for some reason, they did not.

He saw a trainer nearby and asked him why these animals just stood there and made no attempt to get away.

"Well," the trainer said, "when they are very young and much smaller we use the same size of rope to tie them, and, at that age, it's enough to hold them. As they grow up, they are conditioned to believe that they cannot break away. They believe the rope can still hold them, so they never try to break free."

The man was amazed. These strong animals could at any time break free from their bonds but because they believed they couldn't, they were stuck right where they were.

Beliefs can change over time based on experiences and perceptions, which means that even if you believe something as a child, you may not in the future. Like the elephants, how many of you go through life hanging onto a belief, simply because you failed at it earlier?

Let's picture the Tamil classic *Hey Ram*, where a shot of an elephant who mourns the death of his mahout reminded Saket Ram of the loneliness that's going to doom him for the rest of his life.

HOBBIES: ESCAPE FROM REALITY

You may all have different hobbies and even if you have the same hobby as someone else, you often approach it in a slightly different way. Hobbies occupy your mind when you are free. They are your escape from the real world and make you forget your routine. In today's fast and competitive world, your schedule is often very dull and monotonous. Your life becomes an unhealthy cycle lacking any excitement or spark. That is why you need to indulge in something in between to keep your mind fresh and active. Hobbies you a great opportunity to take a break from the routine. They allow you to explore yourself and sometimes allow you to realise the potential you never thought you had.

PERSONALITY

What makes up a person's personality? Their temperament, attitude, thoughts, beliefs, behaviour, and character. Your personality is very unique and it is what other people see when they interact with you. Often people will describe others based on their personality, which shows how special it is. For instance, how many times have you been described as quiet, thoughtful, agreeable, annoying, or rude?

COMMUNICATION

No two people communicate in the same way. The way people communicate reflects their thoughts, beliefs, and personality. Some people are loud and say what is on their minds, while others are more withdrawn and like to keep things to themselves. Some people are excellent at reading body language while others don't see anything past the words coming out of someone's mouth.

GOALS

You all have different desires in life. Even if you have the same type of goal, you often want something slightly different from the next person. For instance, if you have a goal to create a successful business, there can be many different variations from someone else. You may want to make a certain amount of money, or you may just want to influence other people positively rather than make a fortune.

INTUITION

Some people have a high level of intuition that helps them zero in on what they want to do in life, while others need to reason things out before they can decide. While different factors play a part in how intuitive someone is, the brain is one of the big ones. People who have a stronger right brain seem to be more intuitive because they can make a connection between things easily. The right brain is visual and intuitively processes information, while the left brain processes things analytically.

While the neuroscience community doesn't believe that humans operate from solely the left or right brain, there is no doubt that your experiences in life, as well as how you have been taught to approach life, determine how you focus and strengthen one side over the other.

WILLINGNESS TO BE YOURSELF

What makes a person unique? It is their willingness to be who they are and stand out from the crowd. This is a very unique trait because most people are not comfortable embracing their differences and approaching life based on their preferences. Moreover, most people are not willing to show their true personalities and how they would like to interact with the world.

Time and time again, a person will agree with someone else simply for the sake of fitting in. This can happen in the smallest form too. For instance, a person may buy vanilla ice cream, even though they want to buy chocolate ice cream, just so they can fit in. But, it's obvious that even in that little choice they are not happy. They are not in a state of flow that comes with being honest with themselves and others.

RESEARCH ON MINDSET

Carol Dweck, a famous psychologist, and her colleagues have consistently produced results that prove the positive impact of a growth mindset on learning performance.

In one of her early experiments, she ran a workshop for a 7th-grade class at a New York City junior high school. Half the students were given a presentation on memory and effective studying, while the other half was introduced to a better mindset and were told their intelligence largely depended on their effort. After the workshop, both groups went back to their classrooms with their teachers unaware of the difference between what they had been taught.

Remarkably, as the school year unfolded, the students from the second group developed a better mindset and became higher achievers than the students from the first group, who retained a conventional fixed mindset. This theory has shown similar results across different locations, age groups, and subjects with notable degrees of success. In psychology, this mindset was termed the 'Growth Mindset.'

Is it possible to make students develop a better mindset in a 3-hour mindset theory session? If they do so, can they become better achievers?

EMPLOYEE OF THE YEAR

Imagine two people, Sachin and Dhoni, who work in the same company and in the same position. They are of similar calibre and both don't get the promotion they want.

Sachin has more of a fixed mindset about work performance, which leads him to interpret the situation as, "I'm just not good enough" or "My manager will never like me enough to promote me."

Either of these beliefs will likely cause this person to work less diligently. Why bother to work hard if you believe you'll never get rewarded?

In contrast, Dhoni with a better mindset could interpret it as not being good enough yet. Even though Dhoni still likely has a negative emotional reaction, his mindset helped him maintain his integrity.

If a promotion is something they want, who do you think would take action and look for ways to develop their skills? Could the intention that one can improve lead to working harder and likely increase the chance of promotion? Why do you think 10 and 7 are magic numbers?

WHO HAS AN ACCURATE VIEW?

Well, maybe the people with the better mindset don't think they're Einstein or Beethoven, but are they more likely to have sky-high views of their abilities? Will they try for things they're not capable of?

People are terrible at estimating their abilities. People with fixed mindsets are very bad at estimating their performance and their ability. If you have a better mindset, you are more likely to improve since you believe there is hope and opportunity to improve.

When you think about it, it makes sense. If you believe you can develop yourself, then you're open to receiving accurate information about your abilities, even if you need a lot of improvement.

For people with a fixed mindset, everything about their precious traits is either good news or bad news. Unnecessary pressure almost inevitably enters the picture.

Who do you think is more inclined towards learning? Do people with fixed mindsets explore new opportunities if they knock on the door? Do people with better mindsets wait for better opportunities?

RIGID MINDSET

A rigid or fixed mindset is a pattern of thinking that stems from pessimistic beliefs about people's ability to learn, grow, and change their circumstances positively.

A fixed mindset lets you think the purpose of life is about winning or achieving material milestones rather than more rewarding things like transformation or being excited about the journey. It focuses on specific outcomes which will make you far more likely to operate in fear, which brings out your worst self and makes you incapable of enjoying life. It will also lead to an inability to admit your faults and resolve to change.

In a fixed mindset, you consider all of your skills, abilities, and talents as permanent or fixed. You let your entire past determine your future and hand off responsibility to nature or God because you assume that what you have is all you will ever get. Most people destroy their own lives slowly over the years because they haven't addressed this problem in their lives.

People with a fixed mindset don't think these character flaws are urgent because they didn't want to blatantly sabotage their short-term success, so they remain stuck with the usual.

STATEMENTS OF THE RIGID OR FIXED MINDSET

The following are patterns of inflexible thinking that come with a rigid mindset.

- I often get defensive
- Intelligence is fixed and can't expand
- I hate being wrong
- I don't like people who are different from me
- I'm often critical of others
- People can't fundamentally change
- I think very little about how to improve myself
- I'm afraid of making mistakes
- It's hard for me to not hold grudges

♦   Life is happening to me

If you identify with a number of the statements above, then it may be time to start working towards a better mindset. The challenge that arises is that diverse problems require varied responses, yet human beings are especially prone to doing what they're familiar with because it doesn't awaken any fear.

Fear leads to rigid thinking and subsequently blocks abundance. This is how people get stuck in self-doubt, confusion, and stress. Their energy drains away as they dip into despondency and frustration.

GROWTH MINDSET

A growth mindset views intelligence and talent as qualities that can be developed over time. This doesn't mean that people with a growth mindset assume that they could be the next Einstein. A growth mindset simply means that people believe their intelligence and talents can be improved through effort and actions.

In a growth mindset, you believe that your most basic abilities can be developed through dedication and hard work. Brains and talent are just the starting point. This view creates a love of learning and resilience that is essential for great accomplishment. A growth mindset also recognises that setbacks are a necessary part of the learning process and allows you to 'bounce back' by increasing your efforts.

This kind of mindset sees 'failings' as temporary and changeable, and as such, a growth mindset is crucial for learning, resilience, and performance.

With this mindset, an individual excels in challenges and sees failure as a lesson rather than a measure of one's intelligence or mental capabilities.

EFFORT

A growth mindset will see a task as an opportunity to learn. But if you have a fixed mindset you will prefer to delegate the more difficult parts of the task to someone else. In that way, you focus only on easy and minimal work.

CHALLENGE

An individual with a fixed mindset will most likely not want to engage in new challenges because of the fear of failing.

If you possess a growth mindset you will more likely find it appealing and exciting to take on something new and will be willing to master it through trial and error.

MISTAKES

An individual with a fixed mindset will see criticism as a personal attack and feel embarrassed about errors.

In contrast, if you have a growth mindset you will welcome the feedback as it is, whether good or bad and gain insights on the success or failure of the task. You will see the feedback as a push in the right direction.

A growth mindset is a spectacular way of leading your life and should be encouraged from an early age. In the current time, encouragement is a necessity no matter how great or small the accomplishment.

Encouraging students from an early age makes them feel free, comfortable, and relaxed in their environment. Openness is a factor that in itself promotes the growth mindset.

As a youth, you can gain knowledge on this matter quite easily. Technology is now a way of life and has become the new normal of our era.

You can log on to the internet and find books, webinars, and so on to get involved in things. But at the end of the day, it starts from a young age when the schooling system encourages openness amongst fellow students and teachers. It would be a lot easier for the children to adopt the growth mindset.

LEARNING OR PROVING?

The world is not divided into the weak and the strong, or people who succeed and fail. It is divided into learners and non-learners. What on earth would make someone a non-learner?

Everyone is born with an intense drive to learn. Infants stretch their skills daily. Not just ordinary skills, but the most difficult tasks of a lifetime, like learning to walk and talk. They never decide that it's too hard or not worth the effort. Babies don't worry about making mistakes or humiliating themselves.

They walk, they fall, and they get up. They just push forward. What could put an end to this exuberant learning?

As soon as children can evaluate themselves, some of them become afraid of challenges. They become afraid of not being smart and it's heartbreaking how many reject an opportunity to learn. During an experiment conducted among kids in a school, the choices were that they could redo an easy puzzle or they could try a harder one. Even at this tender age, children went with the safer choice.

The kids who believed that they could get smarter thought this was a strange choice. Why are you asking me this? Why would anyone want to keep doing the same puzzle over and over again? They chose one hard puzzle after another.

"I'm dying to figure them out!" exclaimed one little girl.

So the children who chose easy puzzles developed a fixed mindset and wanted to make sure they succeeded. These kids were drawn to the idea that the purpose is to win. Learning is the least priority.

Why did these kids want to win? Why do these kids at an early stage of learning choose easy puzzles? Have schools inculcated the idea of winning by chasing higher grades? Do you think parents have influenced or already placed children in the race?

The kids who chose to do a harder puzzle, tried, failed, won, and then again tried. These kids had a growth mindset and stretched themselves. One seventh-grade girl who chose a tougher puzzle summed it up.

"I think intelligence is something you have to work for. It isn't just given to you. Most kids, if they're not sure of an answer, will not raise their hand to answer the question. But what I usually do is raise my hand, because if I'm wrong, then my mistake will be corrected. Or I will raise my hand and say, 'How would this be solved?' or 'I don't get this. Can you help me?' Just by doing that I'm increasing my intelligence."

Well, most of us would be thinking that would be easy at her age.

STRETCHING

Why do people with a growth mindset seek challenges and thrive on them? The bigger the challenge, the more they stretch. Nowhere can it be seen more clearly than in the world of sports. You can watch people stretch and grow.

Mia Hamm, the greatest female soccer star of her time, states clearly, "All my life I've been playing up, meaning I've challenged myself with players who are older, bigger, more skilful, more experienced—in short, better than me."

First, she played with her older brother. Then at ten, she joined the eleven-year-old boys' team. Then she threw herself into the number one college team in the United States.

"Each day I attempted to play up to their level and I was improving faster than I ever dreamed possible."

What made her compete against players with better skill sets?

Patricia Miranda was a chubby, unathletic high school kid who wanted to wrestle. After a bad beating on the mat, she was told, "You're a joke."

First, she cried, and then she said, "That set my resolve! I had to keep going and had to know if effort and focus and belief and training could somehow legitimise me as a wrestler."

STRETCHING BEYOND THE POSSIBLE

Sometimes people stretch themselves so far that they surprise themselves and do the impossible. Stretching beyond your ability can do all kinds of magic. It will open your mind. It will expand your heart. It will make your soul soar. In doing so, you will be changed and stretched in ways you could have never imagined.

You will come out on the other side more experienced and it is never the same while accepting the challenges. If you are open to it, you will be thoroughly transformed by these experiences. There are learning opportunities buried in the depths and riding in the shallows of every experience. Choose to stretch yourself and watch how your experience of the world mirrors your bravery.

'THE EINSTEIN'

A 21-year-old student studying at Oxford University began to trip and fall, slur his speech and ignored it thinking it was normal. But his father took notice of his condition and took him to the doctor. A series of tests diagnosed Amyotrophic Lateral Sclerosis (ALS), a condition where the nerves that control muscles start failing. He was told that he wouldn't survive for more than two years. No one would have believed he would become the most brilliant theoretical physicist in the history of mankind i.e. Stephen Hawkins. The disease progressed and in a few years he became completely paralyzed, and after surgery on his throat, he lost the ability to speak. For those who are wondering, his curiosity and intellect earned him the nickname 'Einstein.'

In one of his interviews, he mentioned, "My expectations were reduced to zero when I was 21. Everything since then has been a bonus."

However, this didn't prevent him from becoming one of the most eminent scientists of our time. Stephen who couldn't move or talk was able to do wonders and also lead a normal family life with kids.

According to him, he has achieved success thanks largely due to his disease. "Before, life seemed boring. Now I'm happier. The prospect of early death made me realise that life is worth living. So much can be done, and everyone can do so much!"

THRIVING FORCE

People with a growth mindset thrive when they're stretching themselves.

When do people with a fixed mindset thrive? When things are safely within their grasp. If things get too challenging or when they're not feeling smart or talented, they lose interest.

During my college days, most students seemed interested in chemistry. Yet over the semester, something happened. Students with a fixed mindset stayed interested only when they did well right away. Those who found it difficult showed a big drop in their interest and lost their enjoyment.

The mental aspect of not letting yourself down needs to be enhanced. People let go of being successful since they need to learn. People with a growth mindset thrive on such adventures. They need excitement, they see challenges as opportunities.

Is your mission in life 'to survive'? How would your life be if you thrived with some passion and some style?

THE BUTTERFLY EFFECT

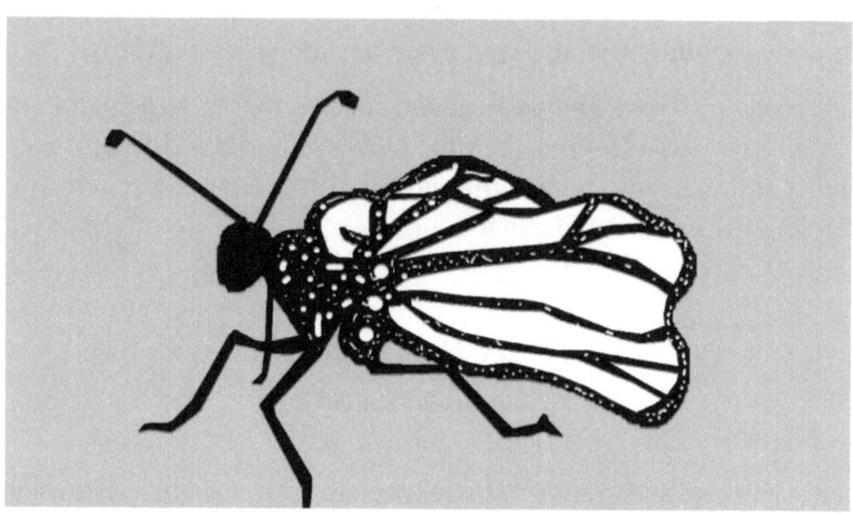

Let's revisit a childhood story.

One day, a man found a cocoon. The next day a small opening appeared in it. He sat and watched the butterfly for several hours as it struggled to force its body through that little hole. It suddenly stopped making any progress and looked like it was stuck.

So the man decided to help the butterfly. He took a pair of scissors and snipped off the remaining bit of the cocoon. The butterfly then emerged easily, although it had a swollen body and small, shrivelled wings.

The man didn't think anything of it and sat there waiting for the wings to enlarge to support the butterfly. But that didn't happen. The butterfly spent the rest of its life unable to fly, crawling around with tiny wings and a swollen body.

Though he had been kind, the man didn't understand that the restricting cocoon and the struggle needed by the butterfly to get itself through the small opening were God's way of forcing fluid from the body of the butterfly into its wings to prepare it for flying once it was out of the cocoon.

Your struggles in life develop your strength. Without struggles, you will never grow and never get stronger. So you need to tackle challenges on your own, and not rely on help from others. When you find yourself cocooned in isolation, you cannot find your way out of the darkness.

It was thought that the events that changed the world were things like big bombs, manic politicians, huge earthquakes, or vast population movements, but it has now been realised that the things that really change the world are the tiny things. A butterfly flaps its wings in the Amazon jungle, and subsequently, a storm ravages half of Europe.

SHOULD YOU STOP LEARNING?

Life is really fun as there are so many different things that can happen to you to make it even better. Nobody knows what is just around the corner. This is the reason why you should never stop learning. Undoubtedly, one of the best opportunities you have in this life is that you can learn many different things. So, there's no reason why you should stop learning, no matter how old you are.

The fixed mindset is when you expect the ability to show up on its own before any learning takes place. After all, if you have it, you have it, and if you don't, you don't. On the other hand, a growth mindset is when you realise that only continuous learning will empower you.

Does learning stop after college? Is learning a lifelong journey?

GENERATING NEW IDEAS

Everything that you have in front of you was once an idea such as mobile phones, the internet, laptops, desktop PCs, vacuum cleaner, etc. Therefore, you can see that everything starts as an idea. So, people need to keep working and learning so they can spawn new ideas whenever possible.

You can continue learning through online courses or any media channel by subscribing to informative resources and more. There are always new skills to learn and strategies for you to adopt.

At the same time, it's of the utmost importance to educate yourself so that you can be inspired by a plethora of different things. Over time, you will be able to create a whole library in your head where you will be able to select from a wide array of different ideas and use them whenever you find suitable conditions. The more you push your brain, the better it works. So, don't stop learning. The fixed mindset does not allow people the luxury of becoming something. They already have to be.

What might inspire your next big idea? This is hard to say, but if you want inspiration to strike, commit to learning something new every single day by reading books, following podcasts, staying updated with the news, or pursuing any number of resources that can expose you to new ideas and concepts. As time passes, you'll begin amassing a mental library of information that will help your brain make connections and keep generating innovation.

Learning is the fuel for this fire!

KEEP YOUR PASSION

A passion gives you a reason to keep learning and to work toward mastery. It can often give you a reason to travel and therefore to have new experiences. It gives you something in common with other people and so fosters social bonds. It may also give you purpose. It gives meaningful structure to your time. It makes the world a richer place. When you're in pain, it can be a refuge, a distraction, or a solace.

Everyone has to face times when their work feels like a chore, no matter how much they love their job. But learning is the key to keeping the passion alive over the long run. Reigniting that passion will only ensure your career remains stimulating. If you want to pursue your passion, you will find ways to enjoy it by simply learning more about it.

What's been a common theme in your life? What skills come to you naturally? What types of things do friends, colleagues, or family usually seek your input for? What would you do for nothing? If you didn't have to worry about money, what would you be doing? What is something that makes you lose track of time when you are immersed in it? What gets your blood boiling? What's a problem in the world that you'd love to fix? What results bring you the most satisfaction?

THE DECLINE OF BOREDOM

Boredom is one of the most dangerous things you can experience during your lifetime. If you've experienced it sometimes, you surely know what I am talking about. In case you want to completely banish boredom from your life, you should commit yourself to constant learning. Without a doubt, this is one of the best ways you can fight it.

If you fall into the trap of boredom, you will be stuck in it for quite a long time. Not having any commitment will only increase the inertia and the feeling of complacency. When you don't take the time to learn, it's easy to get bored.

Who would want that?

Fascination with a particular topic can be engaging and exciting, giving you a greater sense of purpose and excitement in both your career and your everyday life.

What do you do when you feel bored? What kind of things seem boring to you? Do you think young people are more likely to get bored? Why is it that some people work in boring jobs? Why do some people get bored more quickly than others? Do you believe that technology has made life more attractive? Should people make their lives more interesting by themselves?

'JO ROWLING'

One fine morning in 1990, a lady was travelling from Manchester to London by train. She created an entire story from an idea and started developing it during that journey. Unfortunately, her mother died later that year which halted her writing process for some time. But life had different plans for her.

When she moved to Portugal in 1992 to teach English as a foreign language, she met a man, married him and had a daughter. A year later she parted ways with her husband. This was the turning point of her life. She, along with her infant daughter, moved to Edinburgh, Scotland to be near her sister. She had three chapters of the story in her suitcase. It was the most devastating period of her life. She was divorced, jobless, and a single mother of an infant and suffered from severe bouts of depression.

After completing her entire book, she approached several publishers. Not one or two or five, but around 12 major publications rejected the script. She was shattered but not defeated. She kept approaching other publications and her efforts bore fruit.

A small publishing house accepted her book and only 1000 copies were published. Things changed when the book was launched. It was a huge success. The book is Harry Potter and the writer is J K Rowling.

The book has sold more than 500 million copies worldwide and has been translated into 73 languages. It was also adapted into a movie, making it a franchise of a million-dollar business.

It is impossible to live without failing at something unless you live so cautiously that you might as well not have lived at all. In that case, you have failed by default.

ARE YOU WILLING TO FAIL?

From a very young age, you have been taught to be successful. It starts from being admitted into a big school to getting high scores. Every school nowadays has an entrance test even for young children. This is the point where it all starts. If you can get through the test, you will get admitted into a better school thinking you will have a bright future. If you fail, society terms you as a failure. The worst part is you start to believe that you are a failure. Every school and college is the same, the way of teaching may differ but the knowledge you get is the same. What matters is how seriously you take the knowledge and build yourself.

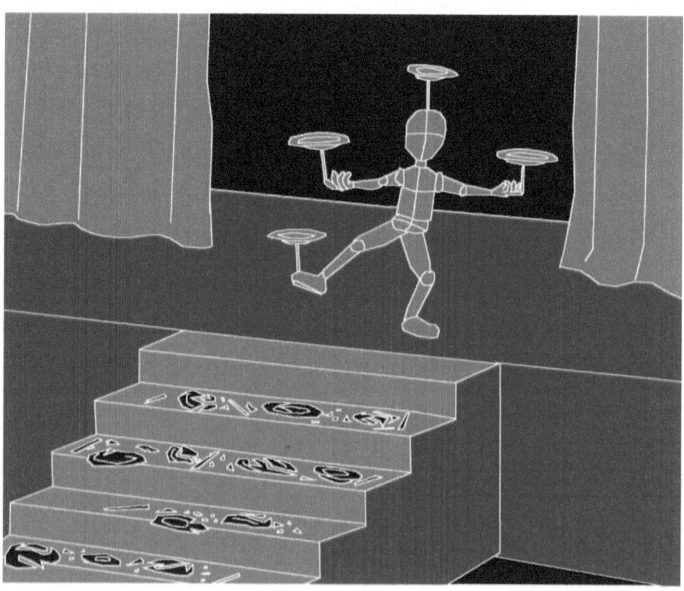

Many people are at the top even though they are from small schools. They didn't feel like a failure when they didn't get admitted into top schools but instead made up their mind and reached the top.

When people with a growth mindset fail, they believe it is an action or a part of their life that got stuck and they can do better the next time and get through. But people with fixed mindsets treat that action as their identity. This attitude will affect your future. Life is full of challenges. If you fail, learn from the failure, try, and repeat.

How is failure usually rewarded at school? Have any failures made your life better? How do you know if you should give up or try harder?

THE BIG RISK

From the point of view of people with a fixed mindset, efforts are only for people with deficiencies. When people already know they're deficient, maybe they have nothing to lose by trying. But if your claim to fame is not having any deficiencies or if you're considered a genius, a talent or a natural, then you have a lot to lose. The idea of trying and still failing will leave you without excuses. It is the worst fear within the fixed mindset.

In the growth mindset, it's almost inconceivable to want something badly, to think you have a chance to achieve it, and then do nothing about it. When it happens, then it is heartbreaking and not comforting for them.

What's the biggest risk you've ever taken? What are the risks in your normal daily life? What is something you would risk your life to get? What are the risks of not taking risks? Would you do a job that was full of risks? Would life be boring without risk? Are risk-takers more successful in life?

"Only a person who risks is free."

Do you think this is true?

ACCEPTANCE

Sure, people with a fixed mindset have read books that say, "Success is about being your best self, not about being better than others. Failure is an opportunity, not a condemnation; effort is the key to success." But they can't put this into practice because of their basic mindset.

Their belief in fixed traits is telling them something entirely different. It says that success is about being more gifted than others, that failure does measure you, and that effort is for those who can't make it on talent.

At some level, people with a fixed mindset don't accept different opinions. They know it all and they always have their say about what someone else should do, say, or how they should look. There is no way you can win an argument with a narrow-minded person, not to mention get to some form of agreement. They will turn the facts around to support their opinion and will never let you have the last word. They have no intention whatsoever of doing anything to improve their situation.

Remember this absurd classroom rule that said, "The teacher is always right?" This was followed by, "If the teacher isn't right, refer to rule one."

LIVING BY STEREOTYPES

You may listen to only one type of music, eat only food from your country even when you travel abroad, see only people within your social circle, etc. There is nothing wrong with preferring one thing over another as long as you're happy. On the other hand, you may miss out on life's different opportunities. A fixed mindset becomes narrow-mindedness. You do that one thing and impose your preferences on those around you.

TOLERANCE

Self-acceptance is a necessary fundamental quality. If you judge your self-worth with what you have achieved, you will be disappointed when things turn haywire. Self-acceptance is the quality of a growth mindset that helps you improve your competence levels.

In today's fast-moving world, people have time for nothing, not even themselves. The modern lifestyle is so demanding that you are forgetting the basics of healthy living that were taught and practised by your ancestors.

You are so preoccupied with your belief systems that, knowingly or unknowingly, you are heading toward self-destruction. The expectations and aspirations of the younger generations are so high that even a small failure pushes the individual into a dark, melancholy world. You can all say that you have accepted yourselves and your lives the way they are but actually, you don't.

Self-acceptance is very important in making the journey of life brighter. It is vital to accept whoever, whatever, wherever you are. Self-acceptance is the process of befriending the unconditioned self, the part of you that is more than just your name, your failures, or your successes.

Accept the way you are first, and then try to work on your faults to improve yourself. Once you find some time to look within, you will find that you have several strengths and weaknesses. Accept them.

Accept your weaknesses and only when you do that you can make efforts to bring about a change. Try to build and maintain your self-esteem. Self-acceptance is the first step toward expressing love for yourself.

In an experiment, couples were divided into pairs and each person was asked to list his weaknesses and the partner's strengths. In all the cases, it was found that the trait listed as one person's weakness was pointed out as his/her remarkable strength by the partner.

For instance, one individual listed anger as his drawback but his partner said that the individual had a dashing presence wherever he went and got his work done every time.

It is a matter of perspective. What you feel is your weakness is your strength in somebody else's view. You don't like yourself because you compare yourself to someone else.

If you are so fond of comparing, practice self-comparison. It will give you a better yardstick to measure progress and chart your growth journey.

DOES SELF-ACCEPTANCE HELP YOU CONTROL YOUR EMOTIONS?

A lack of self-acceptance can affect the part of your brain responsible for controlling your emotions. This can lead to mental imbalance and emotional outbursts as a result of elevated anxiety, stress, or anger. It also limits your capacity for happiness and affects your psychological and emotional well-being. It keeps you focused on your negative aspects and these can create negative emotions. By contrast, high levels of self-acceptance are linked to more positive emotions. Self-acceptance can boost your mood and shield you from the effects of stress and depression. It also helps you create a more positive, compassionate, and balanced view of yourself.

According to Dr. Srini Pillay of Harvard Medical School, acceptance and forgiveness go hand in hand. He says that the inability to accept and forgive ourselves causes us to split into different parts. These two parts need to be forgiven and the one that needs to forgive. Self-acceptance can help you bridge the gap between them, enabling you to forgive yourself for your mistakes and move on. This is essential for your well-being, as dwelling on the past will keep you stuck in the cycle of negative thoughts and emotions.

DOES SELF-ACCEPTANCE GIVE YOU SELF-CONFIDENCE?

Self-acceptance can give you more confidence in yourself. It helps you understand that your perceived negative qualities don't define you or your worth. When you are confident, you are more likely to take action despite your fears. In contrast, a lack of self-acceptance can hold you back and stop you from going after your dreams. Self-acceptance helps you realise that failure doesn't define you and is always a learning opportunity on the path to success. Confidence can also give you greater independence. It allows you to make decisions for yourself without needing the approval of others.

THE MOST TERRIFYING THING IS TO ACCEPT ONESELF

According to researcher Kristin Neff, self-compassion[2] is more important for our mental and emotional well-being than self-esteem. She describes self-compassion as giving yourself 'the same kindness and care you would give to a good friend.'

Anyone who struggles to accept themselves will agree that they tend to be their own worst enemies. Cultivating self-compassion can help you be kinder to yourself when you fail and make you more resilient to setbacks. When you lack self-acceptance, you're constantly trying to hide, censor, or repress your true self. This can leave you feeling drained.

It can help you show up more authentically[3] without worrying about others' judgment. Essentially, when you accept yourself, you feel free to be your whole self.

2. https://self-compassion.org/
3. https://www.betterup.com/blog/authentic-leadership

ARE YOU CREATED EQUAL?

Does this mean that anyone with the right mindset can do well? Are all children created equal? Some children seem to be born with heightened abilities and obsessive interests and through a relentless pursuit of these interests, become amazingly accomplished.

Is it ability or mindset? Was it Mozart's musical ability or the fact that he worked till his hands were deformed? Was it Darwin's scientific ability or the fact that he collected specimens non-stop from early childhood? Prodigies or not, all have interests that can blossom into abilities.

But aren't students sorted into different ability levels for a reason? Haven't their test scores and past achievements shown them what their ability is? Remember, test scores and measures of achievement tell you where a student is, but they don't tell you where a student could end up. No one knows what anyone can do till he tries. Trial and endeavour are the acid test for determining ability.

'Never judge a book by its cover' says the famous proverb and indeed it is impossible to know the contents of a book by merely looking at its cover. One has to read every page and turn it over till one reaches the last page. Similarly, a person would never have found the eternal stone, the diamond, had he not plumbed the earth's subterranean depths.

Though one needs to put one's shoulder to the wheel, endeavour alone will not achieve anything unless it is accompanied by a great mindset and desire.

IS ARTISTIC ABILITY A GIFT?

Despite the widespread belief that intelligence is born not made, when you think about it, it's not so hard to imagine that people can develop their intellectual abilities. You can develop verbal skills or mathematical/

scientific skills or logical thinking skills, and so on. But when it comes to artistic ability, it seems more like a God-given gift. For example, people seem to naturally draw well or poorly.

Society has spread the notion that you must have a natural-born talent for a certain skill, presuming that all it takes is proper genetics to excel at your 'gift,' as opposed to taking adequate time to practice.

But do genetics contribute to our excellence at certain skills or talents? The Indian tennis great Leander Paes has achieved a lot in his glittering career. He won 19 Grand Slam doubles titles and the Olympic bronze in singles at the 1996 Olympics. It was not the first Olympic medal in the Paes household. His father Vece Paes had won the hockey bronze in the 1972 Munich Olympics. How did Leander Paes win a medal in lawn tennis instead of hockey?

Legendary hockey forward Dhyan Chand's achievements will remain eternal in Indian sports history. His exploits on the hockey field won India three consecutive Olympic golds in 1928, 1932, and 1936. His son Ashok Kumar won the bronze medal at the 1972 Munich Olympics. Well, he chose hockey!!

Was Rohan Gavaskar able to achieve glory like his father Sunil Gavaskar in cricket? Should Arjun Tendulkar bet on his father's genes to succeed? Or are these the results of 'practice makes perfect'?

The idea of coming into the world with a natural talent has gone on for generations, most often referring to amazing athletes or musicians that have been good at their talent from the beginning, before even taking the time to practice. However, there is a direct relationship between practice and performance.

With this in mind, it's encouraging to know that even though you may not be the best at something initially, practice can improve your performance, regardless of natural talent. Does this mean that people can control their performance? Can this push them to try something new and take more responsibility for their desires? Is it possible to imagine Goethe or Beethoven being good at billiards or golf?

ONCE THE MINDEST CHANGES, EVERYTHING ON THE OUTSIDE CHANGES ALONG WITH IT!

Your life will be as good as your mindset. It's more important than your inherent ability to learn and has a huge impact on the other areas of life such as career and relationships. All learning strategies, tools, and techniques cannot be enhanced if you don't combine them with a strong, growth-based learning mindset. The simple belief is that the power to improve your learning abilities lies in your own hands, sorry, minds.

How does a person's mindset set the stage for either performance goals or learning goals? A person with a performance goal might be worried about looking smart all the time and avoid challenging work. On the other hand, a person with a learning goal will pursue interesting and challenging tasks to learn more.

The fixed mindset limits achievement. It fills people's minds with interfering thoughts, makes effort disagreeable, and leads to inferior learning strategies. What's more, it makes other people judges instead of allies. Important achievements require a clear focus, all-out effort, and a bottomless trunk of strategies, plus allies in learning. This is what the growth mindset gives people, and that's why it helps their abilities grow and bear fruit.

CHANGING MINDSETS

The growth mindset is based on the belief that you can change. If you've ever had goals and dreams that didn't come true, you're not alone. An incredible 92% of people say that the goals and resolutions they set for themselves each year are never achieved. With stats this high, there must be something in common that's holding them back.

It's important to note that this 8% comes from all walks of life. They can be highly educated or high school dropouts, middle class, wealthy, or even poor by most standards. They comprise a variety of ages and ethnicities from all over the world. The fact is, no matter where you are in life or where you came from, you can set big goals and achieve them.

The brain is like plastic and can be reshaped over time. The growth mindset changes everything because it changes how you look at things. When you change how you look at things, it changes how you feel.

When you change how you feel, you change how you think. When you change how you feel and how you think, you change what you do. When you change what you do, you change your results. Changing your mindset changes your results.

DO YOU FOCUS ON WHAT'S WRONG?

Do you always find yourself worrying and dwelling on disappointments, but never thinking about the things that are going your way? There may be a lot of bad things happening right now, but odds are there are at least some aspects of your life that are in good shape.

If you become blind to the good things, you may lose them, or not use them to your advantage. Do you think figuring out what's going wrong in your life needs a mindset shift? Is it okay to at least find the worst, so you can work it out? Is it critical to examine a negative mindset?

DO UNMET EXPECTATIONS MAKE YOU ANGRY?

Expectations lay the groundwork for your experiences. If you have unrealistically high expectations, nothing will satisfy you. For example, if you set out after college expecting to be a billionaire by age 30 and you find yourself nowhere near that benchmark by that age you will probably be pretty miserable. But are you miserable because you are not a millionaire, or because you have not achieved what you expected to do by then?

You do not live in a perfect world, and even with all the gifts and ambition in the world, you cannot control every factor. But an excuse isn't going to help you anyway. Does the anger fuel and reignite your ambitions? Is there anything that humans should see as unrealistic high expectations? Why can't you control every freaking factor? Is there anything wrong with being successful if you are going the extra mile? Is there anyone to judge you as a freak?

WE'RE LOVIN' IT!

Once, there was an older man who was broke. He was living in a tiny house and owned a beat-up car. He was living off of $99 social security checks. At 65 years of age, he decide that things had to change. So he thought about what he had to offer. His friends raved about his chicken recipe. He decided that this was his best shot at making a change.

He left Kentucky and travelled to different states to try to sell his recipe. He told restaurant owners that he had a mouthwatering chicken recipe. He offered the recipe to them for free, just asking for a small percentage of the items sold. That sounds like a good deal, right? Unfortunately, many of the restaurants did not agree. He heard 'NO' over 1000 times. Even after all of those rejections, he didn't give up. He believed his chicken recipe was something special. He got rejected 1009 times before he heard his first 'YES.'

With that one success Colonel Hartland Sanders changed the way Americans eat chicken and Kentucky Fried Chicken, popularly known as KFC, was born.

Remember, always believe in yourself in spite of rejection.

TIME TO CHANGE YOUR MINDSET

Do you mourn your failure? Do you find yourself feeling angry and desperate whenever you suffer a loss but gloss over your victories? What would your life be like if you don't fail? What is a failure for you? How can anyone expect to win but not be willing to work for it? Do you think failure is underrated?

DON'T YOU WANT TO FACE THE TRUTH?

Complaining about reality is not going to change it. You can rage all day about the rain clouds, but it is not going to bring out the sun. Complaining is a refusal to acknowledge and accept the truth. There are some things you simply cannot change. There is no bigger mistake than refusing to see the real world.

Take action to change the things that you can. Accept that the world will never be fair. Until you can accept that fact and change your mindset, it will never be realistic. The downside of ambition is that it often blinds you to wonderful things and people that you already have in your life. Similarly, you need not settle for less.

Maybe you want a bigger home or a more expensive car, but do you remember the times when you didn't have the home or car you have now? Maybe you wish you had more friends while disregarding the value of the friends you have now.

There is always more to strive for, but due to this, more can never truly satisfy us. It always leaves a hole that is impossible to fill.

Do you need to be satisfied?

DO YOU HOLD ONTO THE DRAMAS OF OTHER PEOPLE?

If the dramas inside your head sound familiar and you catch echoes of voices that are not yours, it is time to let them go. Those dramas belong to those other people and reflect their judgments and perceptions, not yours. You need to put some space between you and the drama.

Why do you care about the opinion of others?

HOW TO CHANGE YOUR MINDSET?

Your thinking needs to adjust. You have all had goals and dreams that didn't unfold the way you hoped or expected. When this happens repeatedly, you start to wonder about what you need to change. But rarely do you look inside at your thinking as the place to start making changes.

You live in a skill-set-driven society that emphasises learning new skills and improving the ones you are weakest at. This often fosters the belief that you need more education to achieve your goals. Some people go back to school, while others take real-life lessons or follow their passion like music, boxing, etc. Always look for that silver bullet among skillsets that will make everything fall into place.

IDENTIFY YOUR COUNTER MINDSETS

Mindsets are formed through prior experiences and emotions. The mindsets that aren't producing the results you want are called counter mindsets which are often fixed.

Some examples of these are self-doubt, limiting beliefs, and any other negative thoughts that get in the way of your fulfilment. Around 65,000 thoughts go through our minds each day. Unfortunately for most people, the majority of thoughts are negative. These 'automatic negative thoughts' occur so often that you're probably not even aware of them.

UNDERSTAND YOUR WHY

Changing your mindset takes work because formed habits aren't easy to break. This is especially true since many of your harmful habits and counter-mindsets were established when you are kids, and you have been doing things the same way ever since. Understanding your why is about starting afresh and deciding on your goal, dream, or mission. When you achieve these, it will signal a transformation.

CAPTAIN COOL

A boy was very fond of playing since childhood. He was initially more interested in badminton and football. His football coach sent him to fill in for the position of wicketkeeper in the school cricket team. He played well and soon bagged a permanent place in the team. This ignited his passion for cricket. He was very passionate about it and wanted to prove himself in the sport.

His father was not very fond of his son's growing interest in cricket. He was of the view that there is no future in sports. However, the boy, whose name was Dhoni, was clear-sighted about what he wanted for himself. He struggled against the rigid opposition from his father for prioritising cricket over studies.

His parents wanted him to join a job that would give him a good earning. He decided to give in and joined the Indian railways as a train ticket examiner in Kharagpur. He had to run all day collecting and verifying tickets at the platforms and, in the late evening, had to sweat out at the training nets. This spirited person worked day in and day out to fight for his passion. He worked to make the most of the opportunities that came his way. He worked half-heartedly as his heart was at the games.

Mahi left his job and admitted that cricket was his only ambition. He wanted to become a professional cricketer. After that, it's the fairy tale of *M.S. Dhoni: The Untold Story*. Dhoni finishes off in style!

In a country where cricket is nothing less than a national obsession and a land where, be it God or the devil, both eat and sleep cricket, Dhoni lifted the bat with a smile.

'Captain Cool' made the country proud with his admirable sportsmanship with all the ICC trophies during his tenure as captain. He believes that the process is more important than the result. The result is just a by-product of the process.

In today's world, if you are so focused on the by-product you may move away from the process. So take care of the process and all the small things. Eventually, you will get the desired result. You may often complain that you should have gotten more as a result, but actually, you got whatever you had prepared for. If you prepare well, you execute well and if you are honest with yourselves more often, you will get the desired result. If there is a shortcoming, then there is always learning.

GROWTH MINDSET IS NOT POSITIVE MINDSET

The growth mindset does not work on expectations. Instead of hoping for the best, the growth mindset works on what is. If the situation does not go according to plan, there is always a reason for it and the growth mindset works on those reasons to pivot and try something new. Hence, there are no expectations in terms of outcomes from the 'experiments.'

THE GROWTH MINDSET WORKS ON FAILURE

Positive thinking eschews failure and focuses on the positives or the successes. The growth mindset is just the opposite. It is not that the growth mindset deliberately tries to fail at everything but it embraces failure because it knows that that is when you learn the most. The growth mindset is cognizant that you don't know what you don't know, and when you fail, you are uncovering what you don't know so that you can enlarge the structural framework of what you do know.

THE GROWTH MINDSET IS A RISK-TAKING MINDSET

The growth mindset is not the gambler's mindset. Positive thinking expects success, it is not geared towards taking risks. The growth mindset will risk being wrong, risk stepping back, and risking one's reputation all in the name of learning and growing.

A growth mindset is not reckless, and will not take unmitigated risks whereas positive thinking stays clear from risks and only expects the best to happen.

THE GROWTH MINDSET IS ACTION-ORIENTED

The output of positive thinking is not specifically to take action, it is to inoculate one's view against the notion of negativity. But in the case of the growth mindset, the focus is on action because it is only in doing that you can uncover the limits of your knowledge and then move towards enlarging those limits.

THE GROWTH MINDSET DRIVES THE HYPOTHESIS-DRIVEN PROCESS

The hypothesis-driven process is a fail-forward mechanism that allows one to fail fast and fail cheaply. The construct is to test the boundaries of what works and what doesn't work, and from there to formulate the right process to move the innovation forward. In contrast, positive thinking expects all actions and activities to be successful. This will cause you to either remain in a process that does not work much longer or avoid the areas where you suspect they will fail, so as to maintain the element of positivity. So a positive mindset is not helpful in an uncertain and ambiguous environment. The growth mindset is very much grounded in reality.

MINDSET - KEY TAKEAWAYS

1. Your mindset shapes the life you lead, the actions you take, and the future possibilities of the world you live in.

2. Mindsets are assumptions people use to make sense of the world. This simple belief can restrict or expand the way in which you engage in life. Your mindset can determine whether you become the person you want to be and whether you accomplish the things you value.

3. People in the same situation could react very differently based on their mindset which dramatically changes their course of action. The view you adopt profoundly affects the way you lead your life.

4. Intelligence, personality and capability are not fixed traits as opposed to the belief that such qualities are carved in stone.

5. If human qualities are things that can be cultivated or things that are carved in stone, then why bother 'trying'? Well, the existence of your mindset answers this query.

6. Your mindset plays a critical role in how you cope with life's challenges. To avoid making mistakes and getting hurt you unintentionally miss life-changing opportunities.

7. The fixed mindset does not allow people the luxury of becoming. Why waste time proving over and over how great you are when you could be getting better?

8. Entering the world of two different mindsets, if you had to choose, what would your priority be—loads of success and validation or lots of challenges?

9. People with a fixed mindset believe that the intelligence and qualities a person is born with will remain the same throughout their life. They do not believe in the power of effort.

10. People with a growth mindset believe that with hard work and experience, growth and development will occur. This mindset

creates a desire to learn. Those with a growth mindset see failure as an opportunity to learn, and they value risk-taking.

11. You try something but it doesn't work, and people may even criticise you. In a fixed mindset, you say, "I tried this, it's over." In a growth mindset, you look to what you've learned.

12. Your beliefs about yourself, other people, the world, what's right and wrong and everything else is never in a million years going to match up to someone else's beliefs perfectly.

13. Intuition is seeing with the soul. When you reach the end of what you should know, you will be at the beginning of what you should sense.

14. The world is not divided into the weak and the strong or those who succeed or fail. It is divided into learners and non-learners. Derive as much happiness from the process as from the results.

15. The passion for stretching yourself and sticking to it, even when it's not going well, is the hallmark of the growth mindset. This allows you to thrive during some of the most challenging times in your life. Sometimes, if you stretch far you may surprise yourself and do the impossible.

16. People are the worst at estimating their potential. There's a lot of intelligence out there being wasted by underestimating one's potential to develop.

17. You like to think of your champions and idols as superheroes who were born different from you. You don't like to think of them as relatively ordinary people who made themselves extraordinary.

18. Effort gives meaning to life. Effort means you care about something, that something is important to you and you are willing to work for it. No matter what your ability is, effort is what ignites that ability and turns it into an accomplishment.

19. People with a growth mindset thrive on adventures. The mental aspect of not letting yourself feel defeated will enhance you.

20. "When you find yourself cocooned in isolation and cannot find your way out of darkness, it is similar to the place where caterpillars go to grow their wings. Courage never goes out of style."

21. You have to be able to accept failure to get better. There is no innovation or creativity without failure. Rejection is neither an indication of value nor talent. Always believe in yourself in spite of being rejected

22. When you change how you feel, you change how you think. When you change how you feel and how you think, you change your action. Your action changes results. Your greatest battle is with your mind

23. If you focus on the by-product you may veer away from the process. So take care of the process and all the small things, and eventually, you will get the desired result. If there is a shortcoming, there is always learning

24. Positive thinking eschews failure and focuses on the positives but a growth mindset dwells on risk-taking, works on failure and is grounded in reality to try something new

25. A growth mindset is a hypothesis-driven approach to failure. It tests the boundaries that work but positive thinking depends only on success which may not be helpful in an uncertain and ambiguous environment

CHAPTER - 4

THE SIEGE

THE EMPEROR HAS NO CLOTHES

Once upon a time, there lived an emperor who cared only about his clothes and about showing them off. He cared nothing about reviewing his soldiers, going to the theatre, or going for a ride in his carriage. Nothing interested him, except to show off his new clothes. He had a coat for every hour of the day, and instead of saying, as one might, about any other ruler, "The King's in council," the people in his kingdom always said, "The Emperor's in his dressing room."

In the great city where he lived, people were happy. Every day many strangers came to town, and among them one day came two swindlers. They were weavers and they said they could weave the most magnificent fabrics imaginable. Not only were their colours and patterns uncommonly fine, but clothes made of their cloth had a wonderful way of becoming invisible to anyone unfit for his office, or who was unforgivably stupid.

"These would be just the clothes for me," thought the Emperor. "If I wore them, I would be able to discover which men in my empire are unfit for their posts. I could tell the wise men from the fools. Yes, I certainly must get some of the stuff woven for me right away."

He paid the two swindlers a large sum of money to start work at once. They set up two looms and pretended to weave, though there was nothing on the looms. All the finest silk and the purest gold thread which they demanded went into their travelling bags, while they worked the empty looms far into the night. Being a bit nervous about whether he would be able to see the cloth, the emperor first sent two of his trusted advisors to see this special material. There was, of course, no cloth at all, but neither of them would admit that they could not see it and so they praised it.

As the word of this special cloth spread, all the townspeople were now interested in learning how stupid their neighbours were. The emperor then allowed himself to be dressed by the con men in his special new suit, made of this special cloth, for the procession through town. Although he knew he was naked, he never admitted it for fear that he was too unfit and stupid to see that he was wearing nothing. He was afraid that the townspeople would think that he was stupid. Of course, all the townspeople wildly praised the emperor's magnificent clothes, afraid to admit that they could not see the clothes, until a child said, "But he has nothing on!"

The child's parents gasped and attempted to silence the child, but the child would not be silenced. As he twisted and turned, pulling his parents' hands from his mouth, he continued to say, "The emperor is naked!"

Soon, a few of his classmates began giggling and joined in. After a while, the adults joined the children and began to whisper, "The kids are right! The old guy has nothing on. He's a fool and he expects us to be foolish with him."

TAKEAWAYS FROM THE STORY

- The Emperor's vanity allows the swindlers to manipulate him. Vanity can lead to the worst of decisions and, specifically, the worst of purchases. And it's also how advertisers persuade consumers to spend money on expensive luxury items.

- The Emperor's pride prevents him from admitting that he cannot see the clothes. The more pride you have, the more difficult it is to admit your fallibility and the more likely you are to allow it to influence your judgment.

- The Emperor's self-importance is boosted by having a whole bunch of obsequious 'yes men' around him. Whether it be an emperor, a president, or a managing director, 'yes men' around a leader can have a devastating impact. If the followers of a leader are unwilling or unable to tell him the truth and stand up to him, then his detachment from reality grows and the leader's belief will soar to levels of conceited self-deception. If no one tells him that he is wrong at times, then he will believe he is always right.

- The tendency to accept 'facts' without question may result in the truth being ignored. The Emperor and the courtiers believe what the weavers tell them and the crowd also believes what their leader tells them in spite of a total lack of hard evidence. All of them assume that the existence of the clothes is beyond doubt.

- Even though everyone can see that the clothes do not exist, no one in the crowd is willing to stand up for the truth. It's so much easier for everyone to just go with the consensus and conform, rather than to think for themselves.

- The child who speaks out, when no one else dares to, is at first exposed to ridicule and scorn. Free thinking individuality and freedom from social conventions can allow the truth to emerge, even if no one else is initially prepared to admit it. This remains true to this day. The innocence of the child is like the man who can see injustice in society to which others are blind. The child reminds us that all of us should have the confidence to speak out.

- Even when the crowd is laughing at the Emperor, he continues his parade. To turn back would be to admit that he cannot see the clothes which would label him as 'stupid.' Though he has been fooled, he carries on, blindly pretending that everyone else is wrong and he is right—the most stupid response of all.

Do you have to believe something because everyone else believes it? Do you think that the school is preparing kids for the real world?

The answer is 'No.'

The school system cannot admit that they are not preparing children for the real world. That would be admitting failure. All of you know what failure means in the school system. It means that your child is not smart. It actually means that the child isn't doing what the school tells him/her to.

Schools are designed on the assumption that there is a secret to everything in life and the quality of life depends upon knowing that secret. These secrets can only be revealed in orderly succession and only teachers can do this. Without financial education, the child will be unprotected once he/she leaves school. He or she might be a topper but they will be parading through life like the emperor.

The problem is that our school system is training our kids to be employees. This is why schoolteachers and many parents continue to say,

"Go to school to get a good, high-paying job." Few parents or teachers are saying, "Go to school to learn to create good, high-paying jobs."

There is a tremendous difference between the skill sets of an employee and that of an entrepreneur. The skills required to be an entrepreneur are not taught in most schools. Many people dream of becoming entrepreneurs, but few take the leap of faith.

In a nation where movies such as *The Wolf of Wall Street* and TV shows such as *Shark Tank India* dominate culture, it's often surprising how many investors google for information on the most basic financial concepts. The lack of financial education is the primary reason why most people remain employees. Without a financial education, most employees are terrified of losing their job, not having a steady paycheck, or simply failing. Financial education and the transformation it delivers are essential for entrepreneurs.

KILLING THE DREAM

Schools seem to have forgotten about the dream. The problem is that the educational system trains students to be academics or bureaucrats. Schools do not train young people to start a business. Furthermore, those who fail to fit into those categories often follow an entrepreneurial path, carrying the torch of capitalism and creating new jobs.

Ask entrepreneurs today and many will tell you that bureaucracies are actively destroying the entrepreneurial spirit. They will also say that many young graduates do not have the skills required for today's work environment.

Modern-day schooling is outdated. Young leaders, innovators, and creators are being turned into robotic machines that follow assignments to generate grades. The grade school years are meant to help students find who they are, but schools today are nothing more than glorified holding facilities for carbon copy education.

Every student has his/her own set of strengths and weaknesses, and yet you find every student following the same academic agenda as their peers. It's almost like schools are asking all students to wear the same size shirt, despite the inevitable variety and differences. An individual with a schooled mind conceives of the world as a pyramid of classified packages accessible only to those who carry the proper tags.

Not knowing what to do during vacations is just proof that society and the school system have stolen your life from you.

SCHOOLING NOT LEARNING

At school, students are taught from day one to blindly follow directions or risk facing disciplinary consequences. The school system was built to match labour environments—eight hours a day with short breaks in a controlled setting to make it easier to push young adults into the workforce.

Schools say that they are preparing students for the future, but they are forcing them to obey commands that expunge all creativity, which is actually robbing students of the ability to pursue a successful future. Students are taught to reject failure, yet many bright and capable students are left behind because their learning style doesn't fit into their teacher's style. Rather than work to help these students understand the material, teachers pass them to the next grade where they can be dealt with, giving these students a false perception of where they stand academically.

When reality finally hits them, it can shatter the students' ambitions for the future and push their dreams into the slow lane. Students are competing instead of collaborating and tearing each other down so they can succeed in a race for rank. Our society has put such a strain on the grading system that kids are pushed to unhealthy limits every day, with teachers that don't teach them according to their individual needs, and with assignments that are often irrelevant to real-life skills. Even though our failing education system won't change overnight, there is a way for students to succeed despite it.

Grades really cover up teaching failures. A bad instructor can go through an entire quarter leaving absolutely nothing memorable in the minds of his class, cull out the scores on an irrelevant test, and leave the impression that some have learned and some have not. But if the grades are removed, the class is forced to wonder about what it's really learning. Several questions such as 'What's being taught? What's the goal? How do the lectures and assignments accomplish the goal?' become ominous. The removal of grades exposes a huge and frightening vacuum.

ENTREPRENEURS DON'T THRIVE IN SCHOOL

Thinking outside the box. Schools expect all students to follow the same curriculum and attend the same classes, participate in the same activities and take the same exams. But in the world of business, being different is sometimes the only way to succeed. People don't succeed as entrepreneurs by doing the same thing everyone else is doing. This approach leaves little room for those with an entrepreneurial mindset to flex their creative muscle and try new things.

Entrepreneurs break the mould and arrive at a solution which no other product or service has been able to offer. That's much more rewarding in an entrepreneur's eyes than acing a subject they'll never use after school. Entrepreneurs learn the knack for coming up with solutions to problems that people aren't aware of. This satisfaction can be much more rewarding for them as opposed to getting a nice grade on their report card.

In school, you attend classes, do assignments and take exams, all in an attempt to earn good grades. Later, what you do with the knowledge you've gained is entirely up to you. However, if you're the kind of person who aspires to use your skills and knowledge for entrepreneurial purposes, the desire to get good grades may pale in comparison to the allure of starting a successful enterprise.

VALUE OF INDEPENDENCE

School is all about doing what others tell you to do—projects, papers, exams and more. Entrepreneurship involves a lot of independent thought and action, which is restricted when you have an instructor waiting for you to hand back an assignment you never wanted to do in the first place. The independence of students who want to be entrepreneurs is stifled in a school setting.

If students are studying a creative practice, they are always under the guidance of an instructor leading them on the 'right' path. Not only that, they are expected to do assignments, in-class tasks and exams on topics that carry no value outside of school. This process can be demotivating, even if you're studying a subject that genuinely interests you.

As an entrepreneur, you develop and exercise the freedom to pick and choose the information that best suits your goals. Plus, you get to see the results on a much wider scale than in a conventional school setting.

SHARK BAIT

During a research experiment, a marine biologist placed a shark into a large holding tank and then released several small fish as bait into it. As you would expect, the shark quickly swam around the tank, attacked and ate the smaller fish.

The marine biologist then inserted a strong piece of clear fibreglass into the tank, creating two partitions. She then put the shark on one side of the fibreglass and a new set of bait on the other. Again, the shark quickly attacked them. This time, however, the shark slammed into the fibreglass divider and bounced off.

Meanwhile, the smaller fish swam around unharmed on the other side of the partition. Eventually, about an hour into the experiment, the shark gave up. This experiment was repeated several dozen times over the next few weeks. Each time, the shark got less aggressive and made fewer attempts to attack the fish, until eventually, the shark got tired of hitting the fibreglass divider and simply stopped its attacks.

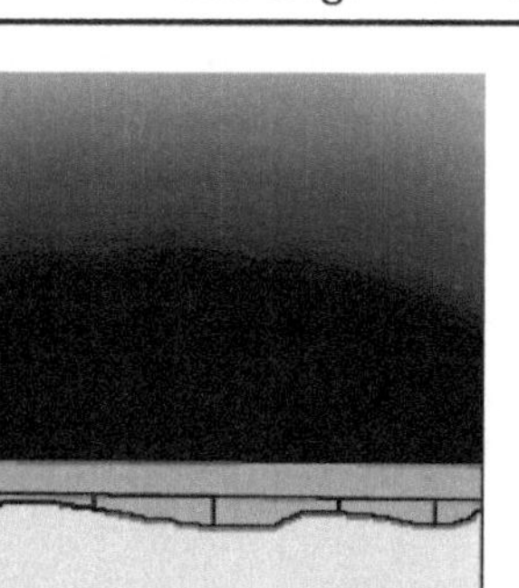

The marine biologist then removed the fibreglass divider but the shark didn't attack the bait. The shark was trained to believe that a barrier existed between itself and the bait, so the smaller fish swam wherever they wished, free from harm.

Schools condition children from a very young age. When they grow up and face setbacks and failures, there is a greater chance that they will emotionally give up and stop trying. Like the shark, you may believe that you were unsuccessful in the past, and you will continue to be so. You may continue to see a barrier in your head, even when no 'real' barrier exists between where you are and where you want to be.

PRACTICAL EXPERIENCE OVER BOOK SMARTS

From junior school to the most prestigious MBA programmes, students are required to read, write, and take tests on hypothetical information. Though some hard sciences may involve practical learning environments, most curricula ask students to think about real-world scenarios instead of becoming involved in them directly.

Entrepreneurs value experience over speculation. They want to get out there and build their knowledge through action, not by studying a textbook. Innovation drives industries to explore new ideas, reach new audiences and create competition in the marketplace.

In school, most of your time is spent learning from others. While it's important to learn the rules before you break them, some people can reach this stage faster than others and you may never get the chance to explore your ideas until you've entered the real world.

Studying real-life and hypothetical scenarios is crucial to developing your knowledge. However, simply bookish knowledge won't suffice within the technological demand that exists in this fast-moving world.

BUILDING CONNECTIONS

Most people outside of school will never ask you about your grades. Entrepreneurs develop their portfolios rather than generating a perfect report card. People should understand the importance of building new relationships, starting new endeavours and putting in the hours to complete projects they're proud to showcase.

If you have nothing to show for your portfolio other than a bachelor's degree or high GPA, you risk being overshadowed by someone with similar qualifications but with financial knowledge. In academia, exposure to good mentors is mostly limited to the classroom. If you're in a class with a lousy or uninspiring teacher, well, then you're out of luck. People who want to learn from the best should go out there to find inspiration. It means stepping out of the school system.

LOVE EDUCATION IN A DIFFERENT WAY

Entrepreneurs are some of the world's greatest risk-takers. As a result, they're students of probability. Going to school won't guarantee future success, so some entrepreneurs may choose to learn in unconventional ways. Podcasts, audiobooks, e-books and online courses involving business, marketing, leadership and so on are more accessible than ever, which means there are plenty of ways to learn outside the traditional school system. Some learning methods are simply more effective at making things happen than a classroom course ever could be.

Schools are about, "How much money can I make?" versus "How much money can I make serving others?"

Schools are about finding a high-paying job rather than creating high-paying jobs. They are about climbing the corporate ladder rather than how to create companies and corporate ladders. They are about job security rather than financial freedom, which is why most employees live in the fear of 'losing their job.'

THE ROCKET MAN OF TODAY

What this man has accomplished so far is nothing short of a marvel. Having inspired Tony Stark in the iconic Marvel superhero, *Iron Man*, he gears up to make the world and beyond, a better place to live in. In today's day and age, Elon Musk holds a unique spot in the present structure of civilisation. The legacy of this Rocket Man has captivated minds all over the planet. The stock market cannot stop talking about him and the younger generations consider him an idol to look up to. Elon Musk, the genius of our time, is yet another engineer who has seized quite distinctive moments in an era of technology and information.

Elon positioned *Tesla* at the helm of the electric revolution. His vision is to embarrass petrol and diesel-run cars and make them seem like horse carriages from the past by crafting the finest climate-friendly electrical vehicles which the world has ever witnessed. Elon envisioned *SpaceX* to aid humans in their evolution to being a multi-planetary species with a civilisation that exists on one planet alone.

Elon believes the current education system could be vastly improved. And it's not surprising. The *Da Vinci* shocks people by saying, "I think school is basically a place to have fun and show that you can do your homework. Separating children by age does not make sense for education, because students have different interests and abilities that are independent of how old they are. Instead of giving children 'tools' in a vacuum, they should be taught how to solve problems. I encourage kids to play since education through games is something natural for them. The philosophy of the school is experimental, not like a traditional old-fashioned school."

INTRODUCTION TO SCHOOL

School is a great experience for children. Every child is a genius. Unfortunately, their genius may not be recognised by the educational system. Their ability may even be crushed. Thomas Edison, one of the great geniuses of modern times, was labelled 'mixed up or confused' by his first teacher. He never finished school and instead became an inventor and an entrepreneur. The company he founded, known today as General Electric, creates products that have changed the world. A few of Edison's early projects were the phonograph, the motion picture camera, and the electric light bulb.

Albert Einstein also failed to impress his teachers. From elementary school through college, his teachers thought he was lazy, sloppy, and insubordinate. Most of his teachers said, "He will not amount to anything." Yet Einstein became one of the most influential scientists in history.

PARENTING

Parenting promotes and supports the physical, emotional, social, and intellectual development of a child. Parenting referred to in this book is obligated to the child's financial, intellectual and entrepreneurial aspects. All parents have met the genius in their child. Most parents know that a child's true genius is found in their dreams. You see glimpses of it from an early age—the ideas and things that delight, fascinate, and challenge them.

Protecting and nurturing the genius in your child is a parent's most important job. Today's parents believe they are helping children by designing each aspect of a child's life. They carefully select not only the school their children attend but also the activities they participate in, the books they read, and the friends they meet. Many modern mothers and fathers closely manage their children's performance by reviewing and correcting homework, speaking to teachers daily, jumping in to resolve a disagreement they have with peers, and hiring tutors and experts to help craft applications for college.

Devoted parents have good intentions and worry that in an increasingly competitive world and a shrinking job market, their children would be left behind and thus, want to do everything in their power to position their children for professional and personal success. However, all the efforts may actually be counter-productive. It is hard to deny that the world our children are going to live in will be demanding. Technological innovation, information overload, shrinking job market, and globalisation all contribute to a world that is much more hectic and uncertain than what earlier generations are used to.

It is not specific knowledge or skill but more conceptual capabilities that would position the young for success. When asked what parents should do to prepare their children for adulthood, the futurist Dr. James Canton's answer was not what most would expect. He advised that children will need the ability to speak multiple languages, live and work in different countries, and effectively deal with change.

In an increasingly ambiguous and uncertain world, success would require adaptability and resourcefulness, which the prevalent parenting approach of micro-management does little to encourage. Instead, parents should incorporate the lessons of the entrepreneur's world to prepare their children for the future.

Successful entrepreneurs have a vision and a mission. To accomplish that vision, they design a bold strategy and implement a practical plan. Company founders are able to visualise both the big picture and the way to get to it. The more parents help children connect what they are doing with the goal they want to accomplish, the more independently children can handle specific responsibilities.

Instead of telling your children, "Put your toys away," and "Complete your physics homework," collaborate with him/her to agree on what goals he/she as an individual want to achieve and then let him/her take the lead on designing the tasks to get to the goals.

Entrepreneurs exercise choice and pursue their dreams more than any other professional. To succeed as an entrepreneur one needs to be passionate about what one chooses. Similarly, if children choose what they want to pursue they will be more likely to be passionate about it, have fun and succeed. Often parents try to push children to be a better version of themselves, compel them to study medicine or engineering, go to the best college or win a specific championship.

Every child has a unique personality. The creative ones love to dance and can convince anyone of anything but hate math. The stubborn ones may never want to get into the pool and learn to swim but love to read books. It is unlikely that anyone would make a mathematician out of the first one and an Olympic swimmer out of the other. But if you let them choose and then guide them, they are more likely to discover their natural talents and become exceptional performers.

No one fails more often than entrepreneurs do. Similarly, children can benefit dramatically from the lessons and strength that come from failing. Instead of resolving every problem for them, let children fail early and often. It is ok to get a less-than-perfect grade, lose a game, scrape a knee, and get into a disagreement with a friend. Small and frequent failures teach children the consequences of their actions, and what effort they need to apply to truly succeed and build their confidence. Teaching children that it is ok to fail as long as they learn from the experience and ultimately improve makes them more resilient and ready for the unavoidable challenges of adulthood.

NOTE FROM 12TH GRADE

"I am a grade 12 student who has graduated recently. You might call me accomplished, and in a way, I am, but not in the way you'd think. Twelve years of pouring over textbooks and being lined up to be judged in front of my peers have not made me any more intelligent. I can tell you the first 45 digits of Pi and I can explain the difference between an acid and a base, I can recite the Pythagorean theorem in my sleep and can recite lines out of a textbook like they are a religion. But I cannot tell you the value of kindness and the distinct contrast between personal health and personal gain.

I can tell you that in grade 10 one of my classmates attempted to take her own life before the finals. I can tell you how when I didn't understand something in organic chemistry, I questioned myself. I was not sure if I was good enough to be there. Memorising became a novelty. Mistakes were viewed as failures in these hallways. A wrong answer is a sin you must atone for, not a human error, but a flaw so grand it defines the entire course of your life.

There is no 'average' here. You must all exceed expectations. Do parents know that a grade that is considered average is a 'C'? When you get a C do you see yourself as lazy and stupid and incompetent? I never fooled around. I am driven by a deep need to impress others. I worked and worked and worked, with a deep hollow of anxiety in my chest. I have never been good at history, but I worked and worked and I attained at best a low B. It was not good enough.

It is not stated openly but you are expected to put your education before your health. It is not asked of you, but it is what you must do to achieve what you are asked to achieve. I've developed a deep-rooted anxiety disorder due to the school and its perfectionist tendencies. Even when you get 99 per cent, it is never good enough. One slip and you are in deep deep trouble."

PEER PRESSURE

There's a dreadful condition that affects parents and strikes when you least expect it. It's not communicable through handshakes or sneezes like the common cold, but in the sneakiest way imaginable, through shared opinions. It's called 'parental peer pressure.'

You're catching up with a friend over coffee when you innocently say, "Mary is really enjoying her break from ballet right now."

"A break?" replies your friend. "Are you sure? We put our little Jyo in a specialized camp over the summer and she's improved sooooo much…"

And there it is, you are the victim of a sudden attack of parental peer pressure.

PUT CHILDREN IN SITUATIONS WHERE THEY NEED TO ADAPT

Today's parents try to provide children with a safe and recognisable environment in an attempt to create a magical childhood. Are parents really doing children a favour or hindering their independence? The world children are about to face is arguably going to be the most dynamic one experienced in the history of human civilisation. Much as the industrial revolution brought an unprecedented level of social, economic and political change, the information revolution increased the speed of the change cycles.

The Blackberry was at the top of the handheld device market for less than 7 years. Can you imagine the rate of change the future holds? Only the most adaptable would be able to manage and succeed in such a world. Consciously exposing children to different situations and giving them new challenges prepares them for the future. One way to do that is to expose them to adventures. Experimentation with new technology can also encourage adaptability. Another way to develop adaptability is to give children room to dream and explore on their own.

Entrepreneurship teaches children not simply how to survive but how to thrive in the face of challenges. The wind extinguishes a candle and energises fire. Similarly, randomness, uncertainty, and chaos energise your spirit. You need to be the fire who wishes for the wind.

If you give children room to experiment and learn while being there for them to love, advise, and guide, they are more likely to grow up better prepared to live productive and fulfilled lives.

LAG TIMES

The problem is that most teachers and parents are products of the same educational system. Many teachers are frustrated and are pushing for change. Unfortunately, the education industry seems to have one of the slowest rates of change.

Different industries have different lag times. One definition of lag time is the delay between the proposal of a new idea and its adoption. For example, in the world of technology, the lag time is around 18 months. This is the time taken between a new idea and its form as a new product. That's why competition can be fierce while bringing a new product to market and why companies soon find themselves out of business because someone else can deliver new products or technology faster, better and cheaper. The industrial age was measured in 50-year increments. The lag time in the information age is measured in 6-month increments.

The reason many teachers and parents are frustrated is that, among all industry sectors, the education industry has the second-longest lag time—50 years. Yet, over time, these sectors will slowly need to climb the ladder of the future.

THE FUTURE OF EDUCATION

The lag time in education means that children starting school today will be grandparents before the educational system adopts the changes this book offers. If lag times hold, it will take until the year 2075 before the newest ideas enter most classrooms.

The truth is you can't afford to wait. Education is becoming more important than ever. Schools provide the important function of training skilled workers to support the economy. For example, schools train doctors, accountants, lawyers, engineers, teachers, social workers, mechanics, police officers, military personnel and others, who are all essential to a civilised society.

Yet, as the global economy sinks into recession, how many of these educated people will find jobs?

Like all learning, financial education is a process that should begin at an early age and continue throughout life. This cumulative process builds the skills necessary for making critical financial decisions that affect one's ability to attain the assets, such as education, property, and savings, that improve economic well-being.

What kind of education is important? Why do you keep telling your kids, "Go to school to get a high-paying job?" Why talk about job security when advances in technology make some jobs obsolete? Why is there so little financial education taught in our schools?

TOP OF THE FOOD CHAIN

Most parents want their children to have a good education for a secure future. They want their children to make it to the top of the food chain. They dread the thought of their children toiling at menial jobs, underemployed, paying higher and higher taxes, and battling inflation all their lives. They hope a sound education will put their child at the top of the class or the leader of the pack—possibly a doctor, engineer, lawyer, or CEO.

THE SALES PITCH

The sales pitch from schools is, "You must finish school. You must have a college degree. If you do not finish school, you will not be successful in life."

The following are 10 people who did not finish school, but that didn't stop them from making it to the top.

1. Steve Jobs, co-founder of Apple

2. Mark Zuckerberg, co-founder of Meta Platforms

3. Bill Gates, co-founder of Microsoft

4. Richard Branson, founder of Virgin Atlantic Airways and Virgin Records

5. Enzo Ferrari, founder of Ferrari

6. Henry Ford, founder of the Ford Motor Company

7. Larry Ellison, founder of Oracle

8. Tom Anderson, founder of MySpace

9. Dhirubhai Ambani, founder of Reliance

10. Most Indian politicians

Once upon a time, all a child had to do was focus on two types of education. They were:

i. Academic or basic education: This education supports the general skills of learning how to read, write, and solve math problems. This is extremely important

ii. Professional education: This education provides more specialised skills to earn a living. The top students become doctors, engineers, accountants, lawyers, or business executives

What was missing?

i. Financial education: This is the level of education not found in the current school system. This is the education of the future. Again, you advise your kids to go to school to get a job and work for money, yet you teach them little or nothing about money

The statistics tell a sad and sobering story that 90 per cent of students want to learn more about money.

BOREDOM

Boredom as a factor in human behaviour has received far less attention than it deserves. It has been one of the greatest motivational powers throughout the historical epoch. Boredom seems to be a distinctively human emotion.

A human would not feel bored while being executed unless he/she has superhuman courage. The opposite of boredom, in a word, is not pleasure but excitement. The desire for excitement is very deep-seated in human beings.

The machine age has enormously diminished boredom in the world. Consider the lower middle-class patriarchal life. In the olden days, after supper, when the wife and daughters had cleared away things, everybody sat around and had what was called a happy 'family time.' This meant women let go of their dreams. They were not allowed to read or to leave the room because the theory at that period was that women were the weaker sex, their goal was to marry, have children, and take care of the family. The world has changed little since then.

Imagine the monotony of winter in the medieval village. People could not read or write, they had only candles to provide light after dark, and the smoke of their fire filled only one room.

Roads were practically impassable so one hardly ever saw anybody from another village. It must have been boredom as much as anything else that led to the practice of witch hunts as the sole sport by which winter evenings could be enlivened.

All this boredom should be borne in mind while estimating the world that existed hundred years ago. When one goes further into the past, the boredom becomes worse.

You are less bored than your ancestors were but you are more afraid of boredom. You think or rather believe that boredom is not part of the natural human life but can be avoided by a sufficiently vigorous pursuit of excitement.

The social shift of allowing women to earn their living has enabled them to seek excitement and to escape 'the happy family time' that their grandmothers had to endure.

Everyone has a membership in Amazon Prime or Netflix—where did the pull come from? Was it a necessity? Compared to the earlier generation Young men and women find it less difficult to meet each other due to their exposure to Tinder.

As you rise on the social scale, the pursuit of excitement becomes more and more intense. Those who can afford it can think of the enjoyment of the nomadic life of ancient men who amused themselves by dancing and drinking. But for some reason, they always expect to enjoy these more in a new place.

Those who have to earn a living lessen their boredom by working. But those who have enough money are freed from the need for work and live a luxurious lifestyle. I am afraid that it is much more difficult for someone in rags to become rich.

Perhaps some element of boredom is a necessary ingredient in life. A wish to escape from boredom is an instinct. Indeed all the races of mankind have displayed boredom as a reminder to explore newer regions. Wars, pogroms, and prosecution have all been part of the flight from boredom. Even quarrels with neighbours have been found better than nothing. Boredom is therefore a vital problem for the moralist since at least half the sins of mankind are caused by the fear of it. However, it is not to be regarded as wholly evil. There are two sorts of boredom, one is pleasant while the other is critical. The pleasant kind arises from the absence of drugs and the critical kind from the absence of vital activities.

I am not prepared to say that drugs do not play a part in life at all. There are moments when the sleeping pill Doxepin will be prescribed by a physician and these are more frequent than ever. But the cravings for drugs are certainly something that cannot be left to natural impulses. A person habituated to drugs suffers from a severe kind of boredom. Once deprived of them, it is like an addiction, and there is no remedy except time.

STONE AGE

Humans are the only known species to have successfully populated, adapted to, and significantly altered a wide variety of land regions across the world, resulting in profound historical and environmental impacts. You can take the person out of the Stone Age, not its impact on the person.

The strength of human beings lies in their minds. The thoughts and emotions are programmed into their psyches and continue to drive many aspects of human behaviour today. In an uncertain world, those who survived always had their emotional radar. The people from the Stone Age were at the mercy of wild predators and frequent natural disasters. Hence, they trusted their instincts above all else. That reliance on instinct undoubtedly saved lives. So for human beings, like for any other animal, emotions are the first screen for all the information received.

CONFIDENCE BEFORE REALISM

In the unpredictable and often terrifying conditions of the Stone Age, the ones who survived were the ones who believed they would. Their confidence strengthened and emboldened them, attracted allies, and brought them resources. They believed they were hard enough to survive and prosper. Thus, people who radiated confidence were those who ended up with the best chances of passing on their genes. The legacy of this dynamic is that human beings put confidence before realism and work hard to shield themselves from any evidence that would undermine their mind games. Belief is another thing that drives life.

CLASSIFICATION BEFORE CALCULUS

The world of hunter-gatherers was complex and constantly presented new difficulties for humans. Which berries can be eaten without the risk of death? Where is good hunting to be found? What kind of body language indicates that a person cannot be trusted?

To make sense of a complicated universe, human beings developed prodigious capabilities for sorting and classifying information. Some illiterate tribes still in existence today have complete taxonomic knowledge of their environment in terms of animal habits and plant life. They have systematised their vast and complex world.

In the Stone Age, such capabilities were not limited to the natural environment. To prosper in the clan, human beings had to become experts at making judicious alliances. They had to know whom to share food with, for instance, someone who would return the favour when the time came. They had to know what untrustworthy individuals generally looked like. Human beings became hardwired to stereotype people based on very small pieces of evidence, mainly their looks and a few apparent behaviours.

DOMINANCE

Along with a scarcity of food, clothing, and shelter, and the constant threat of natural disaster, the Stone Age was also characterised by an ever-shifting social scene. From one season to the next, it was not easy to predict who would have food to eat, let alone who would be healthy enough to endure the elements. The individuals who ruled the clan and controlled the resources were always changing. Survivors were those who were savvy enough to anticipate power shifts and swiftly adjust, manipulate and dominate the clan.

Consider a day in the life of John. He has a charming house and a beautiful family. He wakes up early in the morning while they are still asleep and hurries off to his office. There, he has to display the qualities of a great executive. John cultivates a decisive manner of speech to impress everybody except the office boy. He dictates letters, converses with various important persons on the phone, studies the market, and has lunch with some person with whom he hopes to conduct a deal. The same sort of thing goes on all afternoon. He arrives home, tired, just in time to dress for dinner.

How many hours does it take the poor man to recover from the daily chaotic drama? At last, he sleeps, and for a few hours, the tension is relaxed.

CONTEST AND DISPLAY

Status in the ancient period was often won in public competitions. To establish status in early human societies, people frequently set up contests such as games and battles with clear winners and losers. Likewise, they displayed their status and mental gifts in elaborate public rituals and artistic displays. The underlying purpose of such practices was to impress others. Your challenges may be different from that of hunter-gatherers, but your hardwiring is not.

NIGHT THINKER

When momentary pleasure ends, there is a sense that life is hollow. It is very difficult to escape from boredom in modern life. In the first place, all through working hours, and more so in the time spent between work and home, one is exposed to noise. You learn not to hear consciously, but this may wear you out, all the more owing to the subconscious effort involved in ignoring it.

The instinct of man, as of other animals, is to investigate others and to decide whether one should behave with them in a friendly or hostile manner. This instinct has to be curbed by those who travel in the subway during rush hour, and as a result that they feel diffused rage against all the people. Then there is the hurry to catch the morning train. By the time they reach the office and the day's work begins, the black-coated worker has frayed nerves and a tendency to view the human race as a headache. His employer, arriving in the same mood, does nothing to dissipate it. The fear of being sacked compels respectful behaviour, but this unnatural conduct only adds to the pain.

If once in a while employees were allowed to pull the employer's nose for nearly little benefits but for the employer, whose life is a joker's playground, this would not mend matters. What the fear of dismissal is to the employee, the fear of bankruptcy is to the employer.

If you are someone who takes business worries to bed with you, then in the hours of the night, instead of gaining fresh strength to cope with tomorrow's troubles, you will be thinking about problems over which you have no control. Thinking about problems without producing a sound line of conduct or in a half-insane way will make you an insomniac.

Some portion of the midnight madness will still cling to you in the morning, clouding your judgment, spoiling your temper, and making you crazy. Humans should think about troubles only when there is some purpose in solving obstacles. Go easy on yourself by not thinking at all, especially at night. A great many worries can be diminished by realising the fact that you cannot act on them.

For those who intend to take up public speaking, at first, every audience will terrify you and nervousness will make you speak very badly. It will feel like people might break your leg before you made a speech. Gradually you will teach yourself that it does not matter whether you spoke well or ill, the universe would remain much the same in either case.

It is important to find that the less you care whether you spoke well or badly, the less badly you will speak, and gradually the nervousness will be diminished almost to a vanishing point. A great deal of nervous fatigue can be dealt with in this way.

Your doings are not as important as you suppose. Your successes and failures do not matter very much after all. Even great sorrows can be overcome, troubles that seem as if they must put an end to happiness for life, fade with the lapse of time.

But over and above these self-centred considerations is the fact that one's ego is no longer a large part of the world. The person who can centre his thoughts and hopes can find a certain peace in the ordinary troubles of life.

The psychology of worry is by no means simple. The habit of thinking rightly has its importance, first because it makes it possible to get through the day's work with less expenditure of thought, and secondly, it affords a cure for insomnia.

PUBLIC OPINION

Think about a time when you were extremely anxious, before standing up to speak publicly, raising your hand in a big meeting, or even walking through a room of strangers. The reason you felt small and scared and tense is that you were worried about social disapproval. You care so much about what others think about you because you are living under the assumption that people care about you just as much as you do. Well, my friend, welcome to reality—they don't.

The greatest fear in the world is the opinion of others, and the moment you are unafraid of the crowd, you are no longer a sheep, you become a lion. That bit of sarcasm was intended.

VANITY

"Look at me, look at me," is one of the fundamental desires of the human heart.

There was a priest who, on his death bed, was asked by the disciple if he had any regret in his life.

"Yes," he said, "there is one thing. On one occasion both the Emperor and the Pope visited me simultaneously. I took them to the top of my tower to see the view, and I neglected the opportunity to throw them both down, which would have given me immortal fame."

The stories and world-views you fashion to explain who you are and the world you live in explain your vanity. The completely untravelled person will view all the differences in another herd strangely. But the man who has travelled, or who has studied international politics, will discover that, if the herd is to prosper, it must, to some degree, become amalgamated with other herds.

DO YOU LOVE LISTENING TO FROG CALLS?

A group of frogs was travelling through the woods when two of them fell into a deep pit. When the other frogs crowded around the pit and saw how deep it was, they told the two frogs that there was no hope left for them.

The two frogs decided to ignore what the others were saying and proceeded to try and jump out of the pit. Despite their efforts, the group of frogs at the edge of the pit continued to say that they should just give up and that they would never make it out. Eventually, one of the frogs listened to them and gave up, falling to his death. The other frog continued to jump as hard as he could. Again, the crowd of frogs yelled at him to stop trying and just die. He jumped even harder and finally made it out.

The frog who succeeded was deaf.

90/10 PRINCIPLE

Ten per cent of life is made up of what happens to you. Ninety per cent of life is decided by how you react.

You really have no control over 10 per cent of what happens to you. You cannot stop the car from breaking down and the plane from arriving late, which may throw your whole schedule off. A driver may cut you off in traffic.

You have no control over this 10 per cent. The other 90 per cent is different. You determine the other 90 per cent. How? By your reaction.

Do not let people fool you. You can control how you react.

If you pay less attention to what you are made of, then your talents, beliefs, and values start conforming to what others may think, and you'll harm your potential. You'll start playing it safe because you're afraid of what will happen once you are criticised. You'll fear being ridiculed or rejected. When challenged, you'll surrender your viewpoint and won't raise your hand when you can't control the outcome. You won't take a step forward because you will think that you're not qualified.

Be the chess player, not the chess piece.

Let us look at this from a different perspective. People are different. They differ in their races, castes, creed, religion, languages, and so on. These differences make people think they are inherently different from each other which they are not. At times these differences overwhelm them, make them proud, and settle in their ego. Due to these differences, a person of a given taste and conviction may find himself/herself practically an outcast, rejected by society or certain social groups. A great deal of unhappiness, especially among the young, arises in this way.

Young people somehow latch on to ideas that are present around them but find that these ideas hold only in the particular milieu in which they live. The young feel that the environment they are acquainted with is representative of the whole world. They can scarcely believe that in another place these views would be accepted. The unnecessary task of maintaining mental independence against the surroundings also causes a great dissipation of energy. Thus through ignorance of the world, a great deal of unnecessary misery is endured throughout life.

When you are young, you are surrounded by hostility that teaches the conventional path. If you wish to read serious books and make a change, your teachers may tell you that such works are unsettling. If you desire any career, however respectable, which is not common in the circle to which you belong, you are told that you are setting yourself up for an unworthy life. If you show any tendency to criticise the common notions of politics, religion, education, tradition, and culture you are likely to find yourself in serious trouble. This is why, for most young people of exceptional merit, adolescence is a time of great unhappiness. For all these reasons, people are practically compelled to conceal their real tastes throughout life and they choose to let go of their chance to make a difference.

Public opinion is always more tyrannical toward those who fear it. A dog will bark more loudly and bite more readily when people are afraid of him than when they treat him with contempt. Humans display similar characteristics. If you show that you are afraid of them, you give others the promise of a good hunt, whereas if you show indifference, they begin to doubt their power and, therefore, tend to leave you alone.

WHOEVER CONTROLS THE MEDIA, CONTROLS THE MIND

From its inception, social media has revolutionised the digital world. The spectacular development in communication and innovative entertainment have given people access to information and has given voice to people who would never have been heard. The current generation is fortunate enough to witness some of the most amazing technological developments ever in history.

People always want to connect with society in some way or other. In earlier days, the modes of communication were limited. Earlier, socialising was confined to visiting each other's places, having big gatherings, and meeting in clubs, parks and other public places.

Now, times have changed. People have minimised their social life because of their hectic lives, an increase in geographical distances and economic concerns. With the arrival of technology and social networking websites, people from all over the globe have been brought closer through virtual communities and networks.

Today, every person is addicted to social media and that too at a frightening speed. It has become an integral part of everyone's daily lives. Every day you're bombarded with images of people doing better than you. There is an endless stream of reality shows selling the fantasy that somewhere out there, there are celebrity designers, trainers, and talent scouts helping people just like you lose weight, spice up their wardrobes, or launch music careers.

Of course, you know this isn't how the world actually works. You don't have a makeup team helping you look good, screenwriters coming up with adventures to spice up your day or becoming a billionaire by just watching those clips. But despite knowing that these things are fake, there's still a part of you that wonders why your life isn't more happening and satisfying. This has made social media one of the leading causes of depression and anxiety in modern life.

The productivity of people is getting hampered due to extreme usage and indulgence in these social media sites. When you log into Instagram, it seems as if everyone spends all his/her time having fun. This leads to addiction.

People spend more time on social media, communicating with people all over the world, and consuming content. As a result, they get disconnected from their surroundings.

UNREALISTIC EXPECTATIONS

What you see on social media is the 'ideal' part of a person's life and not their insecurities and problems. When you forget this, you start to compare the negative parts of your life with the eye-catching life of your peers that you see online. In the long run, this impairs your self-esteem. Eventually, you will find it more comfortable to talk on the phone rather than face the person. Do more things that make you forget to check your phone.

DEPRESSION

Depression is a word that is thrown around so easily nowadays. It is used to describe anything from a bad day to an overwhelming inability to live life. But as anyone with depression knows, it is much more than that. It slowly takes over a person's life to the point where they forget how it all began. It is insidious, creeping up and building up over time. Little, unnoticeable things change at first, leading to bigger changes. Then, as if out of the blue, the famous black cloud is overhead.

Depression is when everything feels too hard. When you feel so low that things you previously enjoyed no longer hold the same joy. You wonder how you ever enjoyed anything. You wonder what other people have that you can't get hold of. You find it harder and harder to get out of bed in the morning. You drag yourself through each day. You find it difficult to go to bed at night. Your low is so low that it seems to take over, overwhelming you in a way that you could not have imagined beforehand.

The effort to do even small things is huge. The pressure to do anything is even bigger. People always say you should talk to someone, tell someone, but how do you put something that you find so hard to understand into words?

How do you explain to someone that you want to live your life but also you don't know how you can? How do you explain that this no longer feels like a choice, that it controls you and not the other way around? A reaction to a life that you never imagined would be yours. A reaction to stress and a seeming inability to change your situation. It is a lack of self-care and giving too much of yourself to others. It is a deep anger at the injustice or unfairness of life. It is a lack of energy to take any more of what life has for you. It is deep sadness and regret. It is all of this and much more. You are not always aware of why it happens because of how slowly and quietly it sneaks up on you.

For anyone reading this who can relate to all or some of what I have written, it is no good for me or anyone else to try and make you get help. Yes, at the early stages of depression or mild depression, things like going for a walk, doing something you enjoy or talking to a friend can help. But with a longer-lasting, deeper depression all of these things can feel too hard. This is also what makes it so hard to come out alone.

Allow yourself the time needed to get through this. There is no magic cure, but as slowly as it develops, it can also get better. Before you became depressed, it was hard to imagine what you are going through, now it is hard to imagine ever feeling better.

As impossible as it seems, you need to get help from somewhere, be it your doctor, a professional or the person who is always trying to urge you out of this. None of these people will do it perfectly, but they will support you and you need to allow that. There is always resistance, and sometimes the biggest battle can be choosing to allow others to help.

In case no one else tells you today, let me be the one to say that I love you and I believe in you and your ability to discover your purpose. I hope this gets easier for you. I hope you find a way out of this. I hope you get that sense of control back. Lots of people have been through depression and have come out on the other side. I hope you can find someone who understands what you are going through. Hope is one of those things that disappear with depression, so for now, I will hope for you until you find that hope again for yourself.

THE PARADOX OF EMPTINESS

The experience of emptiness is like no other. Unlike all other emotional constructs where we feel something, feeling emptiness is not experiencing anything. It could be said that this paradoxical human experience sits at the core of all existential philosophies, religious doctrines, and spiritual searches, after all, emptiness, or nothingness is what drives you to know something. But what do you do when your drive is lost and when the absence of all meaning has vanished?

BELLA CIAO

Once upon a time, a psychology professor, Sergio Marquina walked around on a stage while teaching stress management principles to an auditorium filled with students. As he raised a glass of water, everyone expected they'd be asked the typical 'glass half empty or glass half full' question. Instead, with a smile on his face, the professor asked, "How heavy is this glass of water?"

Students shouted out answers ranging from eight ounces to a couple of pounds.

He replied, "From my perspective, the absolute weight of this glass doesn't matter. It all depends on how long I hold it. If I hold it for a minute or two, it's fairly light. If I hold it for an hour straight, its weight might make my arm ache a little.

If I hold it for a day, my arm will likely cramp up and feel completely numb and paralysed, forcing me to drop the glass to the floor. In each case, the weight of the glass doesn't change, but the longer I hold it, the heavier it feels to me."

As the class nodded their heads in agreement, the professor continued, "Your stresses and worries in life are very much like this glass of water. Think about them for a while and nothing happens. Think about them a bit longer and you begin to ache a little. Think about them all day long, and you will feel completely numb and paralysed—incapable of doing anything else until you drop them."

No matter what happens during the day, as early in the evening as you can, put all your burdens down. Don't carry them through the night and into the next day with you. If you still feel the weight of yesterday's drama, it's a strong sign that it's time to put the glass down.

LIFE'S ALGORITHM

The capacity to endure a monotonous life should be acquired in childhood. Modern parents are greatly to blame in this regard. They provide their children with far too much passive excitement such as shows, mobile phones and mostly fast food. They do not realise the importance of acknowledging activities like exercising and the urge to explore which contributes to leading a disease-free life.

Pleasures that are exciting and at the same time involve no physical effort, for example, watching a melodrama in the theatre, should occur occasionally. The excitement is in the drug. Physical passivity during excitement is against instinct. There is also an opinion that a child should be like a plant, undisturbed in the same soil. Too many travels and too many impressions are not good for the young. The idea here is that someone young who has a constructive purpose shouldn't be disturbed by distractions and dissipations.

COMPETITION
DYNAMITE KING DIES!

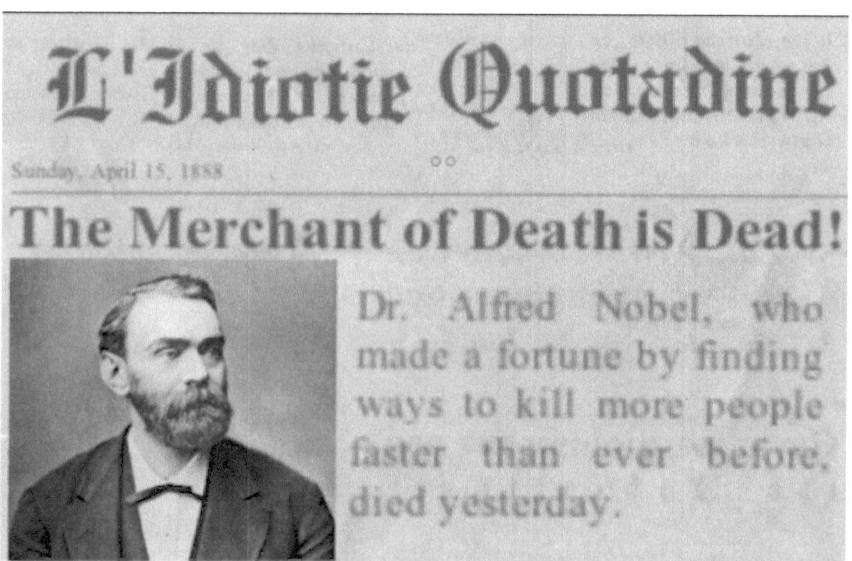

About a hundred years ago, a man looked at the morning newspaper and, to his surprise and horror, read his name in the obituary column. The newspapers had reported the death of the wrong person by mistake. His first response was shock. Am I here or there? When he regained his composure, his second thought was to find out what people had said about him. The obituary read, 'Dynamite King Dies,' and also 'The merchant of death.'

This man was the inventor of dynamite and when he read the words 'merchant of death,' he asked himself a question, "Is this how I am going to be remembered?"

He decided that this was not what he wanted. From that day on, he started working toward peace. His name was Alfred Nobel and he is remembered today for the great Nobel Prize.

Just as Alfred Nobel got in touch with his feelings and redefined his values, do you propose to do the same and redefine your life? What is your legacy? How would you like to be remembered?

Does your society value intelligence, personality, and character? You can see how the belief that cherished qualities can be developed creates a passion for learning. Why waste time proving how great you are over and over again? You can use this time to become better.

Why hide your weaknesses instead of overcoming them? Why look for friends or partners who will just shore up your self-esteem instead of ones who will challenge you to grow?

Your time is limited, so don't waste it by living someone else's life. Don't be trapped by the dogma, which is living with the results of other people's thinking. Don't let the noise of other people's opinions drown out your inner voice. Have the courage to follow your heart and intuition. The passion for stretching yourself and sticking to it, even when it's not going well, is the hallmark of grit and passion.

Sometimes life is like a dark tunnel. You can't always see the light at the end of the tunnel but if you just keep moving you will come to a better place.

SURVIVAL OF THE FITTEST

The survival of the fittest is the ageless law of nature. The fittest are those endowed with adaptation, the ability to accept the inevitable and conform to the unavoidable, to harmonise with the existing or changing conditions. If the most credible 'evolution' and 'the survival of the fittest' is true, the destruction of prey and human rivals must serve as the chief purpose of life. This is also encouraged by human bloodthirstiness, a primitive part of us that is hard to eradicate, especially when a fight or a hunt is promised as part of the fun.

If you ask any sane person what interferes the most with his enjoyment of existence, the reply would be, "The struggle for life." In a certain sense, it is true. In another, it is profoundly false. The struggle for life is really the struggle for success. What people fear when they engage in the struggle is not that they will fail to get their breakfast the next morning, but that they will fail to outshine their peers.

Most often you are caught in the grip of a mechanism from which there is no escape. Sometimes you do not realise this. Your life's algorithm can't run beyond limits. Like drugs, limits exist for every kind of excitement. A life too full of excitement is an exhausting life, in which continually stronger stimuli are needed to give the thrill that has come to be thought of as an essential part of pleasure. The palate of a person accustomed to too much excitement is undermined and dulled by every kind of pleasure. Too little excitement may produce morbid feelings and too much will produce exhaustion. All great books contain boring portions and all great lives have contained uninteresting stretches. A certain power of enduring boredom is therefore essential for a happy life. This must be taught at a young age.

Darwin, after going around the world and paving the way to understanding the existence of life, spent the rest of his life in his own house. Marx, after stirring up a few revolutions, decided to spend the remainder of his days in the British Museum. Altogether in the 19th century, it was a norm that a quiet life is characteristic of great men. Their pleasures were not the sort that would look exciting to the outward eye.

Rich people who already have a good income and could choose to live on what they have, may not do so. It might seem shameful to them, like deserting the army in the face of the enemy. Though withdrawing from the alertness for purpose in life, is to run through the platitudes to be found in the advertisements of the luxury life.

There's no value in suffering when you are doing it without purpose. You desire success and wholeheartedly persuade others to succeed and if you fail to do so, you are a poor creature. Your life will remain too concentrated and too anxious to be happy.

You are a product. You are a product with hopes of a career, relationship, environment and economy of your own volition. The better the choices, the better the product you are—the world judges you based on that simple law. The desire for excitement is very deep-seated in human beings. I suppose that during the hunting stage, it was more easily gratified than it has been since. The chase was exciting, the war was exciting, and the courtship was exciting. Even today, after quite a long period, people chase money, power, fame, and love and continue to remain in the hunting stage.

Human nature has changed little since the time of primitive ancestors. The understanding of the forces which control behaviour, however, has increased immeasurably with the development of scientific methods. Will you succeed or fail? Will you look smart or dumb? Will you be accepted or rejected? Will you feel like a winner or a loser?

Most of you dwell on proving yourselves. Every situation calls for a confirmation of your intelligence, personality and character. Every situation is evaluated. People cannot forget the fundamental instincts of their barbaric past despite their recent space adventures. The fundamental motives that appeal to people are greediness, vanity, revenge and love of power.

THE SIEGE - KEY TAKEAWAYS

1. Self-deception is a process of denying or rationalising away the relevance, opposing evidence and logical arguments The school system is self-deceptive like the emperor without clothes; it cannot admit that it is not preparing children for the real world.

2. Financial literacy is the ability to understand and make use of financial skills like personal financial management, budgeting, investing, managing debt, and financial planning. We have to rethink how to teach financial education in the 21st century An individual with a schooled mind perceives the world as a pyramid of classified packages accessible only to those who carry the proper tags.

3. Schools are designed on the assumption that there is a secret to everything in life and the quality of life depends upon knowing that secret. Landing a man on the moon is much easier than changing the school system.

4. The educational system trains academics and the school system encourages students to take the safe life route that bypasses their dreams.

5. The educational system is incredibly restrictive and recognises only certain types of intelligence. People who are the best outside of the structure get lost.

6. College graduates spent 16 years gaining skills that will help them command a higher salary, yet little or no time is spent helping them save, invest and grow their money. People with low financial literacy are unable to take their ideas and create assets from them.

7. Test scores and measures of achievement tell you where a student is, but they don't tell you where a student could end up. Schools are about climbing the corporate ladder rather than how to create companies and corporate ladders. Young leaders, innovators, and creators are being turned into robotic machines that follow assignments to generate grades.

8. The school system was built to match labour environments. Schools teach children from day one to blindly follow directions. Learning can only happen when a child is interested or else it's like throwing marshmallows and calling it eating.

9. Entrepreneurship is living a few years of your life like most people won't so you can spend the rest of your life like most people can't. Entrepreneurs don't thrive in school.

10. Job security is a myth in this techno-recession era. The driving force of a career must come from the individual. Remember, jobs are owned by the company, you own your career. It is better to take full responsibility for your financial situation instead of depending on a job.

11. Lag time is the delay between the proposal of a new idea and its adoption. Different industries have different lag times. The education industry has the second-longest lag time—50 years. Yet, over time, the education sector needs to climb the ladder of the future.

12. If parents want to give their children a gift, the best thing they can do is to teach their children to love challenges, be intrigued by mistakes, enjoy effort, and keep on learning. That way, their children don't have to be slaves of praise.

13. True self-confidence is the courage to be open to change and new ideas regardless of their source. Real self-confidence is not reflected in a title, an expensive suit, a fancy car, or a series of acquisitions. It is reflected in your mindset. Your readiness to grow.

14. Life is a fight against boredom and emptiness. The fundamental motives that appeal to people are greediness, vanity, revenge and love of power.

15. "Look at me" is one of the fundamental desires of the human heart. False glory is the rock on which vanity is wrecked. The knowledge of thyself will preserve thee from vanity.

16. Your time is limited, so don't be trapped by the dogma of living with the results of other peoples' opinions. Don't let the noise of others'

opinions drown out your inner voice. The more opinions you have, the less you see.

17. Ten per cent of life is made up of what happens to you. Ninety per cent of life is decided by how you react. You've control over 10% of what happens to you. You can always choose how you react to every situation, it's your attitude that will allow you to power the 90%.

18. Social media from its inception has revolutionised the digital world with the illusion of connectivity. We live in a world of ghosts. We are all half-present for most of our day. Nowadays, whoever controls social media controls the mind, which causes depression and anxiety.

19. Public opinion is tyrannical. How many of you have read history, shaken your heads, puffed your chests, and said, "If I were alive during that period, I would have never done those things to those people!" Yet here we are, doing those things to others.

20. Distinguish melancholy from depression. 'Steal' some time and give it exclusively to yourself. Opt for solitude. You don't need to reject the rest of the world but you need to breathe. Depression can cut all the flowers but cannot keep spring from coming.

21. Emptiness is a paradoxical human experience that rests at the core of all existential philosophies, religious doctrines, and spiritual searches. Ultimately, the drive is lost after finding the meaning of life.

22. You are a product. You are a product with the hopes of a career, relationship, environment and economy of your own volition. The better the choices, the better the product you are—the world judges you based on that simple law.

23. People find out what they want to do in life and chase after greatness to prove to themselves that they are great at what they do. With time, they realise they don't need anybody's approval, as doing what they want to do gives them purpose, and fulfilling that purpose gives them a satisfying and meaningful life.

24. The survival of the fittest is the ageless law of nature. The fittest are those endowed with adaptation, the ability to accept the inevitable and conform to the unavoidable, to harmonise with existing or changing conditions. So, we're just prisoners of adaptability.

25. If the most credible 'evolution' and 'the survival of the fittest' is true, the destruction of prey and human rivals must serve as the chief purpose of life. This is also encouraged by human bloodthirstiness, a primitive part of us that is hard to eradicate, especially when a fight or a hunt is promised as part of the fun.

Image Illustrator - Joseph Prince

Cover Designer - Komal Telagavi